Auca on the Cononaco
Indians of the Ecuadorian Rain Forest

Text and photographs:
Peter Broennimann

Birkhäuser Publishers
Basel · Boston · Stuttgart

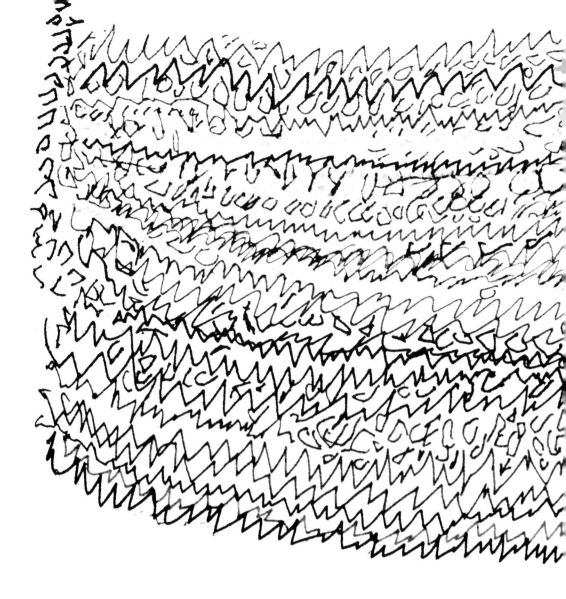

Peter
Broennimann

Indians
of the Ecuadorian
Rain Forest

AUCA

on the Cononaco

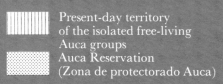
Present-day territory
of the isolated free-living
Auca groups
Auca Reservation
(Zona de protectorado Auca)

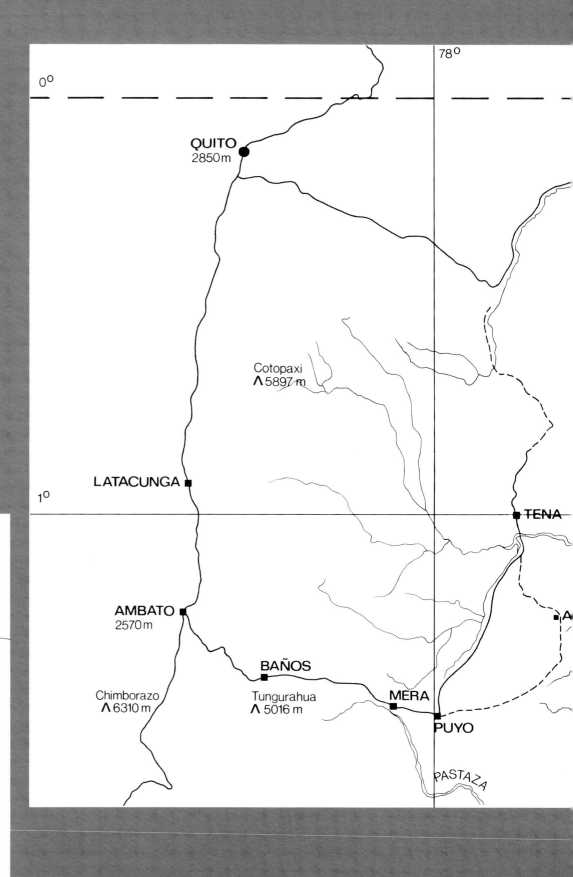

ECUADOR

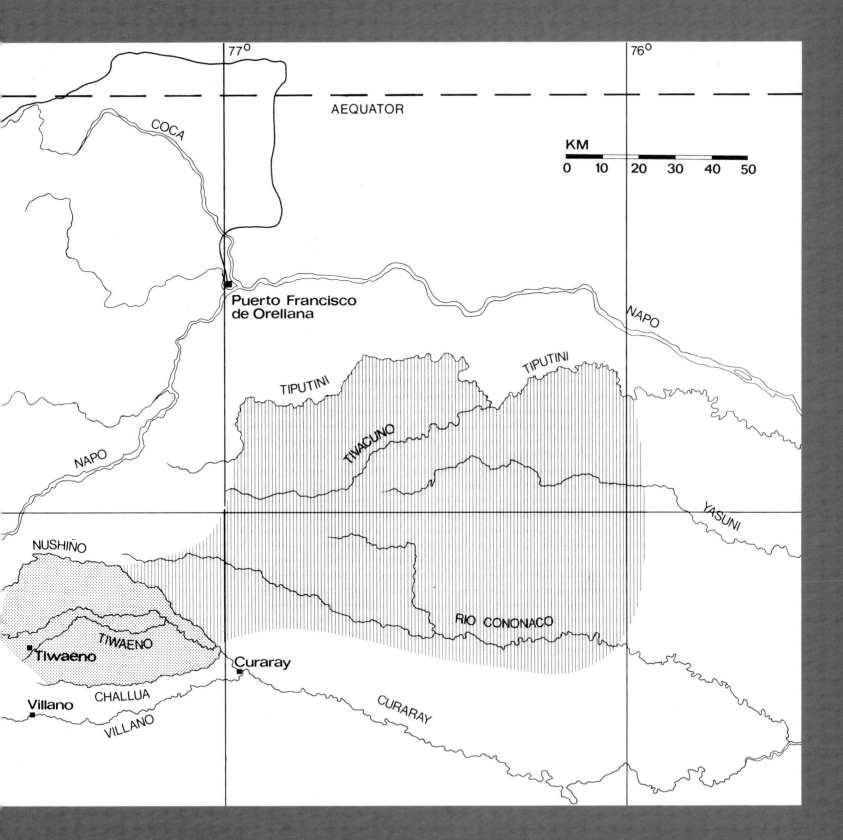

AEQUATOR

KM

0 10 20 30 40 50

77°

76°

COCA

Puerto Francisco
de Orellana

NAPO

TIPUTINI

TIPUTINI

TIWACUNO

NAPO

YASUNI

NUSHIÑO

RIO CONONACO

TIWAENO

Tiwaeno

Curaray

Villano

CHALLUA

CURARAY

VILLANO

Library of Congress Cataloging in Publication Data

Broennimann, Peter, 1924–
Auca on the Cononaco.
Title on added t.p.: Auca am Cononaco.
Includes index.
1. Araucanian Indians.   I. Title.
II. Title: Auca am Cononaco.
F3126.B76   980'.004'98   81-9972
ISBN 3-7643-1259-9   AACR2

CIP-Kurztitelaufnahme der Deutschen Bibliothek

Broennimann, Peter:
Auca on the Cononaco : indians of the Ecuadorian rain forest / Peter Broennimann. –
Basel ; Boston ; Stuttgart : Birkhäuser, 1981.
Dt. Ausg. u.d. T.; Broennimann, Peter:
Auca am Cononaco
ISBN 3-7643-1259-9

English version: Eileen Walliser-Schwarzbart
Layout and design: Albert Gomm
Printed by Birkhäuser AG,
Graphisches Unternehmen, Basel
Printed in Switzerland
ISBN 3-7643-1259-9

Cover photo
The luminous red toucan feathers shine in magnificent contrast to Menga's blue-black hair. Free, proud and content, he lives in harmony with nature in the tropical forest of his forefathers. But his freedom is endangered. Oil companies and missionaries see only the 'primitive heathens lost in the realms of darkness' and will be able to find no peace until the last Auca is on the reservation.

Title page
Menga's first drawing: carefully and conscientiously he has put one line next to the other and deliberated over his choice of colors. Visibly pleased with the results, he explains his work: "Those are trails that run through the forest, and big huts and many Auca with blowguns."

Contents

The author with Cincawae

Sam Caento Padilla, the son of an Auca and a Spaniard, is a man between two worlds. For the Linguists who educated him he is nothing more than a lost hope today. But for the Auca on the Cononaco he is an important link to the outside world.

The Auca's huts stand above the Cononaco, far removed from civilization. The interrelated group of twenty-six, made up of Menga's, Apa's, Boca's and Caruae's families, live in close harmony with nature here in the tropical rain forest.

The excitement over our arrival has not yet died down. As the first white woman on the Cononaco, Wally becomes the focal point of their curiosity again and again. We are struck by the Auca's small build. At an average height of 1 m 54 cm, the men are about 10 cm taller than the women.

> Gami belongs to Titae's group. In contrast to Cacadi's features, hers carry only a faint trace of the Mongoloid stamp. Months later she fell victim to the Linguists' promises. On the Tiwaeno Reservation, the Auca pay for their guileless curiosity with their freedom. The first thing the zealous missionaries taught naked Gami was a sense of shame.

Innocent of clothing, they wear nothing but a hip-cord. The Mongoloid element in Cacadi's features is unmistakable. She is in the early stages of her first pregnancy.

Auca huts are solid and rainproof.
Under the palm-thatched roof, which slopes
down from the high ridge beam to the
ground, the usual confusion reigns: a jumble
of hammocks hanging round the fires, plaited
baskets, carrying bags, spears, blowguns,
kapok containers and bamboo quivers
everywhere.

>
Awaenca is proud of her child. Healthy and
well-fed, it will spend the first years of its life
in the constant loving care of its mother.

Introduction

Still almost untouched by civilization, the last free Auca live in Ecuadorian West Amazonia, where the foothills of the Cordilleras flatten out into tropical rain forest. Their traditional territory, an area of more than 10,000 square kilometers, lies east of the 77th meridian, extending from the sweeping arc of the Rio Napo in the north to the Rio Curaray in the south.

Their way of life has changed little since their ancestors migrated from Asia across the Bering Strait to America many thousands of years ago. In the isolation of the jungle they have remained semi-nomadic hunters and gatherers. Their history is obscure, and their ethnic origin and linguistic family are still matters of speculation.

The Auca believe that theirs is the only true world. They call themselves 'Huaorani', or people. Anyone else is a 'Cuwudi', a strange being from an unapprehended outside world. 'Auca' is actually a contemptuous Quechua term for jungle barbarians; but the name has so firmly taken root that it can hardly be avoided today.

Forgotten by time, the Auca attracted worldwide attention in 1956, when five young North American missionaries were slain by their spears. The image of 'Stone Age savages who hate all strangers and live only to hunt, fight and kill' was reinforced, and they were decried as 'the worst people on earth'. The inaccessibility of their native environment and their hostile view of the outside world have made them the ethnographically least known forest Indians in South America.

Their survival is endangered. The number of free Auca who have been able to assert their independence up to the present day by militantly rejecting any attempts at domestication has dwindled to one hundred. Five hundred that have already been 'pacified' and missionarized live on the Auca reservation on the headwaters of the Rio Curaray.

Auca:
An Endangered
Tribe

The Auca are a unique phenomenon because they provide newspaper headlines while remaining among the least known South American Indian tribes. Both famous and notorious, decried as spear murderers by missionaries and journalists alike, they share a dubious reputation for animal savagery with the Jivaro and the Waika (Yanomamö). There is a great deal of literature written by anthropologists and accessible to the layman on the two latter groups, which could balance the distorted image propagated by the media. But our information on Auca culture is based only on very tendentious reports by the Summer Institute of Linguistics (SIL) or superficial descriptions by journalists.

There are various reasons for this dearth of in-depth ethnographic studies. Until about twenty years ago, the Auca managed to avoid contact with the outside world. Their isolated life in the hinterlands of the Napo and Curaray rivers of the Ecuadorian Montana and their determination to defend their territory against intruders by armed force may have frightened off any number of researchers. Another significant factor is the mistrust many Latin American governments harbor against anthropologists because the governments fear they might have an inhibiting effect on national development and integration policies. As the aims of Christian missions (and that includes Protestant ones) coincide much more closely with those of the respective Catholic administrations, close cooperation between the two often results. In eastern Ecuador, which is considered a particularly neuralgic point because of its borders with Colombia and above all with Peru, the predominance of certain very efficient missionary societies are promoted to such an extent that they can practically control a region of this kind with government approval. There is no room for freedom of research here. Those in power are more prepared to tolerate tourists, considering them the lesser evil.

The fact that our knowledge of these people consists of scraps and half-truths is due to this combination of economic, geopolitical and spiritual interests on the one hand and the Auca's hostile isolation on the other.

The Auca are not a people without history, as has often been maintained. Their culture and way of life are dynamic and have changed over the centuries, too, but not the way ours have and not in a way comprehensible to us. As in the case of most of the Indians of the tropical rain forest, their past is unknown. No one knows how many centuries or millenia the Auca have been living in the region between the Napo and Curaray. For one thing the habitat offers almost insurmountable obstacles to archaeological research; then, too, their material necessities

of life, which are mainly of plant origin in the jungle and thus ephemeral, make the reconstruction of cultural continuity far more difficult.

As a people without a written language, they pass down their tribal history orally from generation to generation. These myths, which tell of the creation of the first Auca and of the great flood, cannot be interpreted either temporally or locally. They elude the research of our historians, who therefore scorned this type of '(hi)story' for such a long time, banishing it to the realm of fantasy. So one-sided and ethnocentric a mentality denies existence to all phenomena that do not fit into our system.

But we, for example, lack terms for kinship and genealogies that go back more than two generations and/or encompass more than two families; in present-day linguistic usage, for instance, we no longer distinguish between maternal and paternal uncles or grandparents. But precisely those peoples without a written language have developed an ingenious vocabulary for this, also historical, purpose.

It was only when the Andean countries were conquered by the Spaniards that their Indian inhabitants entered European historical awareness and that chroniclers also informed us of the events during the period of Inca rule. At that time the Inca Tupac Yupanqui (c. 1418–1482) is supposed to have tried to subjugate the Auca, the 'wild' forest Indians on the other side of the eastern Cordilleras. In vain. His military campaign did, however, promote the spread of the Inca language, Quechua, which consequently replaced the languages of some of the Montana tribes completely. From then on, the word Auca, which means 'warlike, wild, hostile' in Quechua, was used by the Spaniards as a collective term for all nomadic, non-Quechua-speaking and later for all non-Christianized tribes of the east. This fact has rendered the identification of the groups mentioned in Spanish sources with the Huaorani-Auca difficult to this day.

In 1539, Francisco de Orellana left Quito to go east in search of the gold of El Dorado. Travelling down the Napo to reach the Amazon and finally the Atlantic, he was probably the first European to cross Auca country. Even if the Auca were already living in the inaccessible hinterlands and not on well-frequented waterways, news of the strange white man must have reached them. But it was only in 1640, when the Jesuits charged with missionarizing the east established permanent settlements, that the Spaniards were able to gain a firm foothold. Quechua became the general, colloquial language down to the Amazon. When the Jesuits

were expelled from Latin America (1767), their settlements on the Napo and Curaray also fell apart. The priests had united all kinds of Indian groups like the Zaparo, Encabellado, Abijiras, Oas (Huaorani-Auca under another name possibly among them) in such mission villages to keep them under better control. For almost a century the Indians enjoyed a certain isolation, since the missionary societies that followed did not have the same potential at their disposal as the Jesuits, and the wars of independence against the Spanish mother country with the ensuing postwar confusion absorbed the Andean states' attention.

But with the growing demand for rubber towards the end of the 19th century, the Amazonian rain forest suddenly became a focus of economic interest, which led to a proper 'rush' of india rubber collectors, merchants and settlers in the area. It brought the native population contagious diseases, death, slavery and dependence on the white man. Demographic movement and migrations resulted. Thus in the 1920's, for example, the Auca started migrating to a region formerly inhabited by Zaparo groups, as the latter had almost completely died out in consequence of their contact with 'civilization'.

All too soon the rubber boom was followed by oil prospecting, which proved successful in eastern Ecuador. At the same time, missionary activity was intensified after World War II, with the American Summer Institute of Linguistics in its fanatic zeal and technical superiority soon proving more effective than the Capuchins, who had traditionally operated in the territory.

The Auca rightly saw their territory being threatened on all sides by the approaching front of civilization. They retreated as long as they could, but when the foreigners started invading their territory more and more frequently, they began defending themselves. It is disturbing to realize that we, who talk so much about freedom and human rights, show so little understanding for this struggle for survival – not only physical but psychic survival. The attitude of the 'cuwudi' of today seems frighteningly similar to that of the Spanish Conquistadors and the American pioneers. The fate of the Auca is not unique. There are many other South American Indian groups who have lived in the tropical rain forest of Amazonia for thousands of years and are experiencing the same thing today.

A characteristic of the peoples living on the jungle-clad eastern slopes of the Andes, the so-called Montana, is their linguistic variety, which is unique for South America. Apart from representatives of larger linguistic families, like the Tukano, the Pano and the Aruak (later immigrants), we find a great many small or even isolated linguistic groups. The Auca, whose linguistic family is still in dispute, may belong to one of the latter.

The cultural range of the Montana peoples is as varied as their languages. To make a gross generalization, we might say that the Auca represent one particular type of tropical forest culture. It is characterized by a semi-nomadic way of life, small local groups of patrilinearly extended families, and technical equipment which is relatively simple but perfectly adapted to the environment. Sweet manioc, plantains and bananas grown by slash-and-burn agriculture and palm fruits which are collected when ripe form the basis of their diet. Their need for protein is met by game hunted with the lance or the blowgun, a masterpiece of precision and, among the Auca, of unique, flat, oval shape. Fishing with fish poison (and lately with fishing rods) plays only a minor part.

Although most of the Auca's calories probably come from the gardens cultivated and tended by women, hunting, with its aura of danger and the unpredictable, enjoys much greater prestige. A good hunter is a successful man (and popular with women, too). He does not just feed his own family; he feeds the whole local group because he has to divide up his kill according to certain rules. The central significance of the hunter for the welfare of the group also manifests itself in the ideologies of peoples of this kind. One could almost talk of a 'hunting mentality'.

One of its elements is the balance between nature, which is considered animate, and human activity – a balance that must be re-established again and again. The hunter, for example, asks the animal lords, to whom all game belongs, for permission to kill; through ritual activity, he tries to compensate for the loss or even to increase the number of animals. The interpretation of dreams, tabus (e.g. eating tabus) as well as accidents, diseases or unsuccessful hunting expeditions, all of which are thought to be punishments meted out by offended animal lords, regulate relationships with the environment and function as ideological controls over the exploitation of vital resources.

For these people the jungle is not a 'green hell' to be fought and conquered. On the contrary, they see it as a source of satisfying their needs. It gives them everything they need to live: food, clothing, ornaments, raw materials for homes and tools of all kinds.

The depletion of the tropical soil as well as the migration of game leads to periodic movement from one area to another within a certain territo-

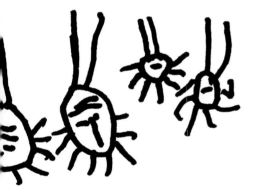

The Auca stand on both banks of the Cononaco in Boca's drawing. He has placed himself, his wives Awaenca and Giicabae and their five children in the middle. The larger figures at the upper edge of the picture are Cuwudi, strangers from beyond the Rio Napo. When asked for the names of the people drawn, he was disappointed that the 'lettering' at the left edge of the picture had not been understood.

ry. As recent scientific studies have shown, the rain forest needs at least ten, normally fifty and under adverse conditions over a hundred years to regenerate. The Indians, with the experience of centuries in dealing with this complex environment, are correspondingly careful. This means that relatively few people (in our case, formerly 600 Auca) needed a comparatively large area to live in – about 13,200 sq.km. Survival in the traditional style is not possible on a reservation with fixed, closely drawn boundaries (today 525 Auca live on the only 1007 sq.km SIL reservation); decisive structural changes necessarily result, and they, in turn, do not remain without effect on the ecological system. Moreover, inter-ethnic and domestic tribal feuds between members of various local groups can also cause single families or whole groups to move away. To remain mobile, which is desirable for the reasons mentioned above, groups must be kept relatively small. Like other Indians with a similar way of life, the Auca limit their population by practicing birth control as well as infanticide; if what the missionaries say is true, the frail and the sick who endanger the functioning of the group are also killed. In accordance with their circumstances, their definition of life differs from ours. Thus in many cultures, small children who are not yet initiated and/or have no name yet are not considered proper persons. It is only through rites of passage, the time and character of which depend on ecological and social factors, that a child is introduced into the role that society has intended for him and thus into 'actual' life. Death, too, is seen and explained differently. Supernatural powers like the wandering souls of the dead and dangerous spirits are the prime movers behind disease and death. But often the blame is also put on malevolent members of outside groups (these may be other ethnic or other Auca groups), mainly the shaman (sorcerer-priest/medicine man), who has special powers. He can, for example, harm his 'victim' or steal the latter's soul with the help of invisible objects. This is always fatal unless the shaman of the victim's own group takes counter-measures. The shaman's 'profession' is respected because it is feared, but it is also dangerous, as revenge for misfortune tends to be taken on the 'medicine man'. Another cause of disease and death lies in not heeding prohibitions and in the infraction of tabus. It is precisely the spiritual background of such beliefs, the Auca's view of the world and their system of values that we know next to nothing about. As the example of other forest Indians, who have been the subject of thorough ethnological research (e.g. Jivaro, Yanomamö, Tukano tribes, etc.), shows, they have differentiated, logically constructed systems of thought and belief which guarantee social coherence and help the members of a society to accept their economic and political roles. This knowledge is an absolutely necessary prerequisite to understanding Auca culture.

But without the linguistic 'key', "what holds their world together deep down" remains inaccessible. Thus the present volume is not a scholarly monograph in the anthropological sense. But it offers more than the thrilling story of two people's experiences, because it gives us insight into the everyday life of the few (approximately 100) 'free' Auca, i.e. those not on the SIL reservation. The book does not perpetuate prejudices and clichés, nothing is sensationalized or transfigured. Instead, the reader is invited to participate in an impressive encounter of two cultures in which one can sense respect and understanding for an alien way of life. Speculation and misinterpretation have been consciously avoided. The impressions speak for themselves, and where the author analyzes the Indians' situation, he does so on the basis of well-founded knowledge of Latin American conditions gathered over many years. It is to the author's credit that he tries not only to show the problems with which the Auca are confronted but to seek possible solutions. For there exists a widespread, fatalistic view – even among anthropologists – that forest Indians are in any case doomed; and it is all too easy for this view to serve as a false justification for dangerous indifference or to be used against these fellow human beings.

One need not agree with the solutions offered. They are probably not easy to realize. Certainly the land question will become increasingly important, as is the case everywhere in Amazonia; and title to the land, guaranteeing the Auca their rights to their territory, is among the most urgent demands. It might be very difficult to find a 'common denominator' because the Auca have a fundamentally different grasp of such concepts as 1) possession – the Auca are not familiar with individual territorial property, 2) the economic system – the Auca use their environment to cover their basic needs and do not exploit it for a market, 3) administration – as an egalitarian society, the Auca have no political leaders; their family groups function independently and autonomously. Moreover, their mental attitude is diametrically opposed to ours. This is where the anthropologist, thanks to his training, could intervene, as a sort of 'translator' from one culture to the other. There are prejudices to be broken down and misconceptions to be corrected on both sides. The representatives of our culture must gradually begin to realize that there

are many ways of living in a community, that the form we have chosen is not the only valid one, that other societies have achieved things unknown to us, and that we could learn a great deal from them and their wealth of experience. Conversely we are obliged to prepare people like the Auca for what they will encounter in a world that has become alien to them. They must be shown the consequences of adapting themselves to our way of life, things must be put into perspective, advantages and disadvantages clearly shown. But ultimately there is no outside group, no matter how well-meaning, that can decide for the Auca what they want their future to look like. As the example of the Jivaro-Shuar shows, Indians are as capable as we are of taking their destiny into their own hands. And we should learn to accept the fact that these ideas and plans may look completely different from what we had hoped and that the Indians are not here to fulfil the white man's dream.

Annemarie Seiler-Baldinger

Boca intuitively expresses the visual impressions of his world. He has an explanation for every detail: apart from portraits of Auca and strangers, he has drawn monkeys, birds, snakes, anteaters, sun and stars. In the middle row one can recognize an Auca father resting in a hammock with his child.

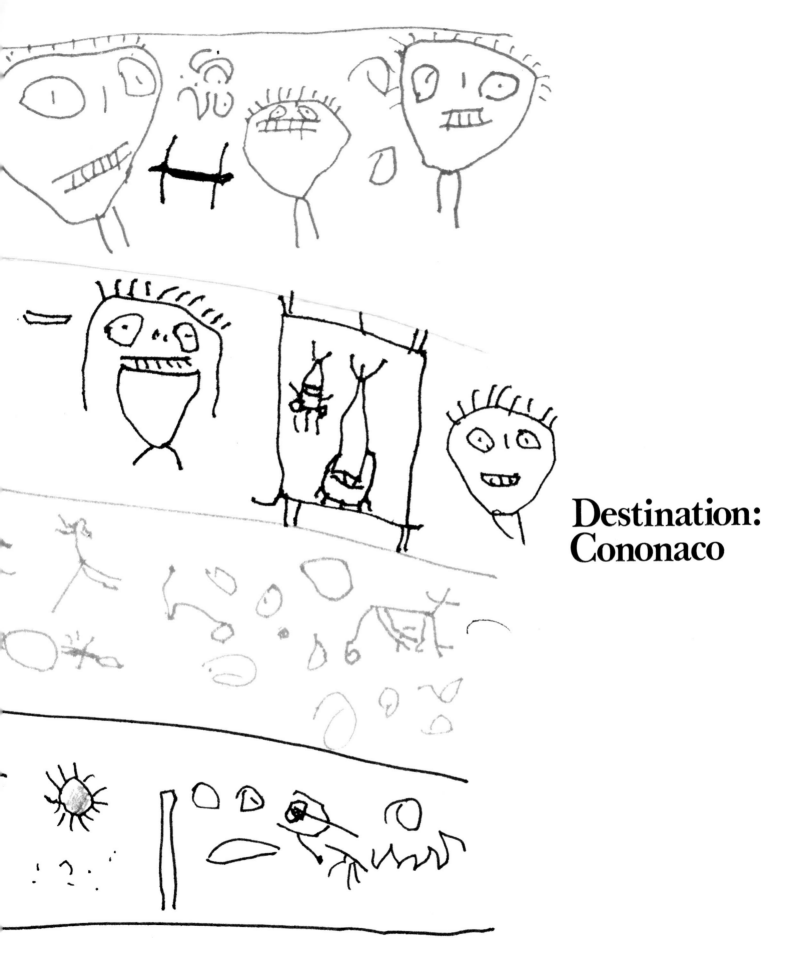

Destination:
Cononaco

On a clear October morning our bus shakes its way from Quito to Ambato. The road stretches across the Sierra plateau, through the Cordillera Mountains, past Latacunga, past eucalyptus forests and dusty, poverty-stricken Quechua villages, past Indios in coarsely-woven ponchos, their faces hard, their expressions blank, and past endless cactus hedges white with dust.

Our destination: the Auca on the Cononaco.

Sam had given us the key to a small clearing lost in the green wilderness of the Ecuadorian rain forest. Just a few weeks earlier, our enterprise had seemed hopeless. The only reactions to be encountered on the word 'Auca' were fear and prejudice. There was no one in Quito who could or would lead us to them; they would take us to the missionarized Auca who had been bundled off to the Tiwaeno Reservation, or to the Cofán on the upper course of the Aguarico, or even to the notorious Shuara, better-known as Jiváro, long famous for shrinking the heads of their enemies. But to the last Auca living free in the isolation of the jungle in their natural state – never. No reasonable person seeks contact with them voluntarily, even taxi drivers in Quito know that.

Until we met Sam. We waited for him over bullshots and guacamole at the Colon Bar, Quito's traditional meeting-place. He found us through the confusion of chairs and voices: "Hi, I'm Sam." After only a few minutes he had captivated us; people like that are rare. Slim, medium height, sharply chiseled features in an intelligent, dark-skinned face: the unmistakable stamp of an Indian. Bushy brows and beneath them dark, almost melancholy, eyes revealing nothing, yet lighting up unexpectedly when he laughed. An Indian nose; thick, widely curving lips; blue-black hair parted over his forehead and hanging down long and straight over his shoulders.

Sam Padillo, whose Auca name is Caento, is the son of Dayuma and a Quechua[1]. Brought up by American missionaries, he speaks English, Spanish, Quechua and Auca. We had heard and read a great deal about Dayuma[2]. Thirty years before, at the time when intra-tribal killing was sowing fear and death, she had been the first Auca to leave the protection of the forest. Moipa, feared and hated by all, and his band of Auca had been threatening Dayuma's group. Hardly a week went by without someone being speared to death; not even women and children were spared. When even Dayuma's father, badly injured by a spear, was buried alive by his own people and her mother threatened in despair to kill her own children, Dayuma could no longer stand it. In spite of her

1 That was the missionaries' official version, as it later turned out. Sam's real father is Vicente Sevilla, the son of Don Carlos, the hacendado. To cover up this embarrassing business, Dayuma's marriage to the Quechua Miguel Padilla was arranged in 1950.

2 Ethel E. Wallis, 'The Dayuma Story, Life under Auca Spears' and 'Auca Downriver' (Wycliffe Bible Translators).

To go on an expedition in eastern Equador, one needs a lot of patience. We are waiting for a more favourable weather report in the hangar of the Missionary Aviation Fellowship in Pastaza. In the background, the Cessna that got us to the Cononaco on our second attempt.

terror of the Cuwudi, the uncanny strangers living on the other side of the Rio Napo, she decided to flee. It was on Don Carlos Sevilla's hazienda 'Ila', where she found refuge and married a Quechua who died of measles shortly after Sam's birth, that her path fatefully crossed that of Rachel Saint, a North American evangelist missionary.

Although Rachel's brother, Nate Saint, had been one of the five Wycliffe missionaries killed by Auca spears on the Rio Curaray on that January day in 1956, the unfaltering Miss Saint felt she was destined by God to spread the Gospel to the heathen murderers, whatever obstacles she might encounter. In Dayuma she found a willing tool for this purpose. Dayuma helped her to decipher the language; and in 1958, Saint and Dayuma, who had by then become a God-fearing servant of the only true church, had their first unbloody encounter with a group of Auca. But more of that later.

It was easy to see that Sam did not think too highly of the Wycliffe Linguists. Again and again he had tried to frustrate their plans and keep them away from the free-living Auca, who were retreating further and further into the forests. He knew of a relatively large group that had since the beginning of the year been living at a spot on the Rio Cononaco where seven years before a French prospecting firm working for Texaco had built a small, rudimentary airfield in the wilderness, only to give up the project and leave the field to be reclaimed by the jungle. The airstrip was, he said, threatened by encroaching undergrowth – not a strip for beginners to practice on, but an experienced bush pilot would have no trouble. The Auca had happened upon the runway during one of their hunting trips. They just saw it as a clearing in the forest; and with the river nearby and the slight elevation above, it suited their idea of a good place to live. As there seemed to be plenty of game in the area, they decided to stay and built their huts above the river.

Sam had already visited them there twice, though only briefly. He had met some of them before, and thanks to his origins and knowledge of their language, he was successful in breaking down their initial mistrust. On his second visit, accompanied by the Commander of the Ecuadorian Air Force, whom he hoped to gain as an ally against the Linguists' plans, he took along gifts that finally broke down their resistance for good.

Sam was ready to lead Wally, my wife and staunch companion on all my adventures, and me to the Auca on the Cononaco. Now he is dozing on the seat of the bumpy Expreso Oriental. Every time the constant shaking makes his head slide off his green army duffle bag, he opens his eyes in tired slits, laughs or curses and makes a fruitless attempt to go to sleep again.

In Ambato we find a taxi-driver who, after a short bout of bargaining, agrees to take us to Puyo in an old, worn-out Chevrolet proudly sporting a Mercedes star on the hood. The road winds higher and higher through small, stony plots of corn and potatoes. Now and then we catch a glimpse of the Tunguraha volcano. Small, barefoot Salasaca mountain Indians, faces leathery beneath their light, broad-rimmed hats, trot along the road in short comic steps. They are wearing black ponchos and greyish-white shirts and trousers. A final climb and then one narrow steep bend after the other, down into the Matate Valley, where the first palms and banana trees immediately indicate the beginning of a different, tropical world.

The Rio Pastaza still foams wildly between the rocks here, and overhead large black clouds move across the pale blue sky. After Baños, where Nuestra Señora de Agua Santa is still said to work miracles, the first heavy raindrops begin splashing onto the dusty windshield. Beyond Baños the road becomes a real adventure. It cleaves to the steep slopes in narrow bends. Torrents gush unexpectedly across the rocks and drum on our metal roof. Narrow wooden bridges without railings groan and sway. Waterfalls crash down to the Pastaza between wild blue hortensia bushes. The fog, only patchy up to now, thickens into a dense blanket of gloom, and rain starts pelting down. Ghostly headlights appear ahead. We can just barely make out the silhouette of a truck and avoid a collision by a hair. Rivulets swell into dirty streams and flood the road, and we glide though the yellow mud as if in a dream. But our driver is as calm as can be and has no trouble getting us safely though the deluge.

Finally the rain stops. Pallid sunlight shines through the rising fog. The jagged rocks have flattened out into hills green with thick vegetation. In Shell-Mera or, as the natives call it, Pastaza we stop briefly at a military checkpoint, and a short time later our long drive to Puyo is over.

Puyo, an unbelievably rainy place, is the last outpost of civilization in the province of Pastaza. For whites, Quechua and mestizos from the surrounding settlements and hamlets it is a shopper's paradise at the edge of the jungle: you can find anything there – from refrigerators, radios, colorful clothes and cheap jewelry to machetes, fishing hooks, aluminum pots, parrots and shrunken sloth heads. The showers in the bungalows of Joe Brenner's Turingia even work, and we can bask in the luxury of hot water. Joe, an American of German descent, is a unique combination of adventurer, hotel-owner, famous orchid breeder and barterer of Indian ornaments and pottery. He only knows of the Auca from hearsay, but over a drink he has plenty of stories to tell us about the atrocities they have committed. Sam listens in stoic silence.

Early morning in Shell-Mera, and we have already received permission for our flight, signed by Señor Coronel Comandante de Pastaza personally. Now we are waiting for Capitán Romero. At nine o'clock it starts to rain – planes do not take off in the rain here. The scheduled flight to Villano, Macas, Curaray and Arajuno has already been delayed for two days. The passengers sit on benches waiting: a Quechua nurses her child; her husband, a hunting rifle wrapped up in his lap, sits next to her gazing into space; a dark-skinned girl with big black eyes is playing with a woolly monkey; a missionary in a white cassock and spectacles is asleep, an open book in his hands; and two young bearded Israelis are about to lose patience.

At eleven o'clock the weather begins to clear, but there is still no trace of Romero and our plane. A piercing siren announces the arrival of a two-engine army Noratlas. At lunchtime there is a commando group from the Twentieth Bush Brigade making mock war on the road. Suddenly they are here with automatic rifles, the faces beneath their steel helmets blackened with soot. The young lieutenant takes everything very seriously. His orders are brisk: assault, stop, take cover. They fight their way up the deserted street, house by house, ultimately disappearing into a sidestreet as if the whole thing had been an apparition.

Again the siren announces the arrival of a plane, and this time it is the 'Chupisopla' with Capitán Romero. He is not enthusiastic about our flight. He refuses to make any promises: "Con este tiempo ... pués, no sé ... veremos" and points towards the east, where the clouds are still almost black near the horizon. "It would be the Auca they want to visit!" we hear him mutter. He says he will make up his mind after lunch.

It is 2 p.m. The bright sun robs Romero of his last excuse for a delay. We drag Wally away from her soup. Our luggage is weighed. Permission for take-off. The engine starts and we taxi across the road to the airfield. Minutes later we are winging our way in a great arc over the tea plantations on the Pastaza, flying over Puyo and climbing higher above undulating hills that ultimately flatten out into the great stretch of jungle. Here and there we can still see haziendas, an occasional clearing and a few huts by the river; then traces of settlers become sparser and sparser, and finally, beyond Villano, there is nothing but forest and rivers.

The luxuriant wilderness of the tropical rain forest extends as far as the eye can see. Thousands of trees closely woven into one green carpet rolled out to meet the horizon. The Rio Villano meanders in golden serpentines, giant blossoming trees scatter prominent splashes of yellow, mauve and orange among the uniform green, and small swamps glitter in the sunlight like mirrors strewn about the jungle by an invisible hand. After half an hour we are flying over the Curaray, and the northern sky has darkened. On our left a bad-weather front, turbulent and black as night, drives billowing, leaden clouds and wave-like veils of rain towards us. On our right, in the south, the sun still glares against a background of deep azure. We fly east through the arc of a rainbow, over nameless rivers and then – there is the Rio Cononaco! Downriver we cut across its brown meanders and look for the small rectangle of a runway, for huts and clearings in the ocean of trees. Nothing. We fly lower towards what looks like smoke curling upwards, but it is only a patch of fog caught in the treetops.

Romero consults his map, glances nervously at the clock, checks the fuel gauge and says that we must have missed the runway. Despite our protests he wants to change course. Suddenly we see an ochre strip shining up through the green near the river: the runway! Romero takes the machine down, heading it straight towards the narrow, irregular bit of ground. The first flight over already shows us that the northern flank of the forest, with bushes and saplings, has narrowed the central part of the runway down to barely fifteen metres and that dirty puddles of rainwater glisten everywhere. We see a hut on a slight elevation at the end of the flat field and in front of it the indistinct outlines of two tawny figures: the Auca!

Sweat is streaming down Romero's face: "No es posible. Asi no puedo aterrizar. – The runway is wet and overgrown. I am not going to risk my life for those damned Indios."

"We have to land! Por favor, Capitán!"

"Okay, I'll try it again."

Is he afraid? Is he right? Don't people say that bush pilots have developed a kind of sixth sense in judging jungle runways?

A second attempt: skimming the treetops with throttled engine. Near the ground now, trees so close you could touch them through the windows. Now! But Romero does not dare to land, accelerates again and the plane begins climbing. Minutes later, speechless, we are over the forest flying westwards. Exactly two-and-a-half hours later we are at the Shell-Mera airport again[3].

3 Capitán Romero was killed in an air crash over the jungle in October of the following year. In the wreckage, the fuel tank of his 'Chupisopla' was found empty and the valve to the second tank closed.

In the pouring rain Cincawae returns from hunting with a howler monkey he has bagged.

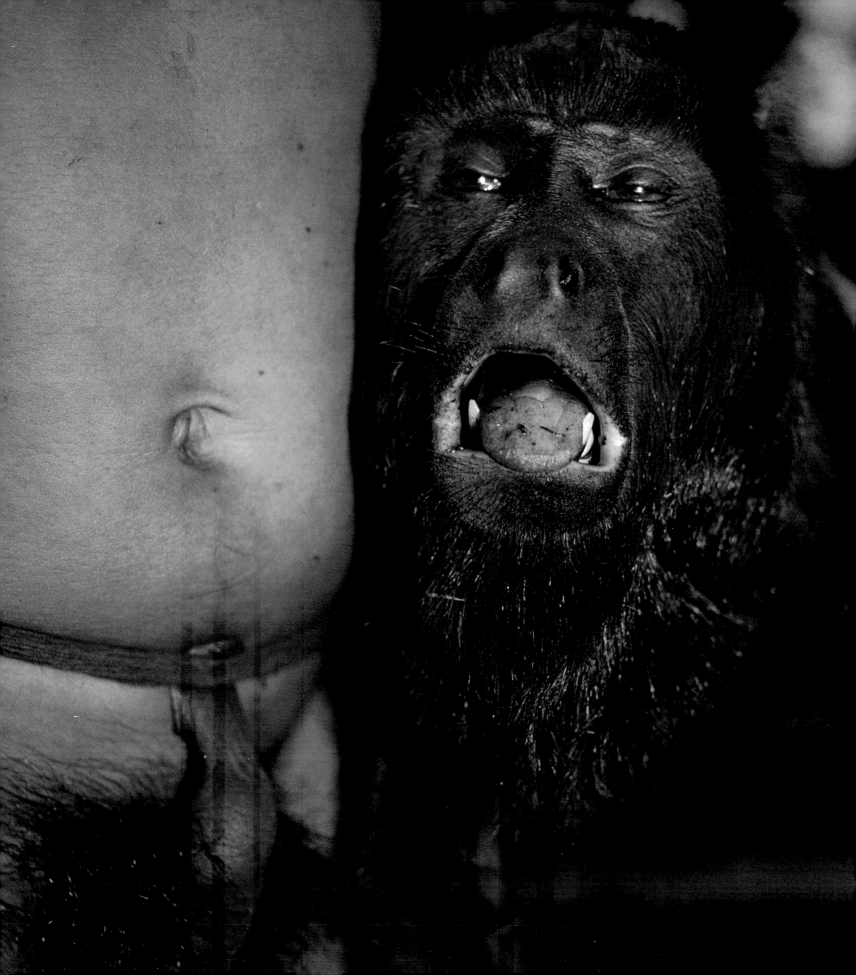

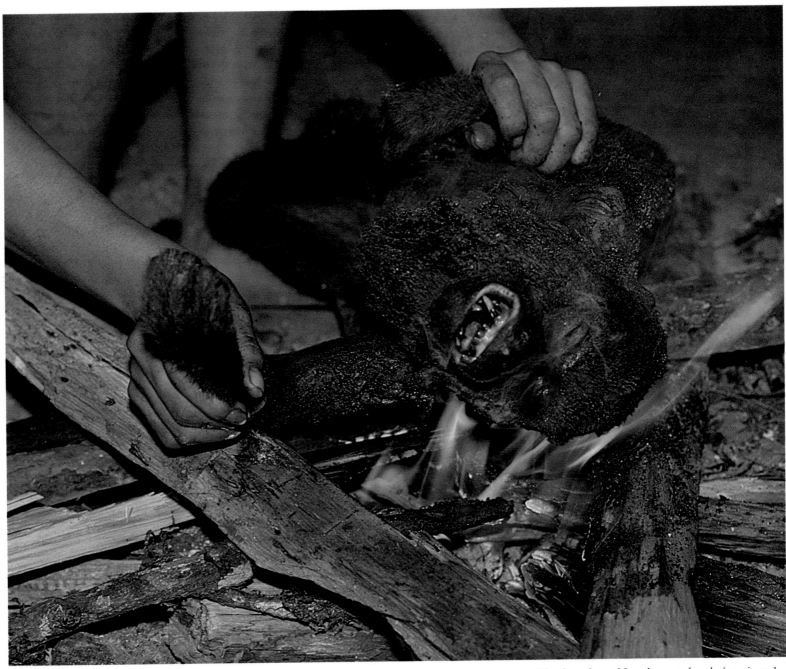

The fur of a red howler monkey being singed. Monkey meat is the Auca's most important source of protein. It is cut up into fist-sized pieces and boiled, unseasoned, in water until tender. Salt is unknown to the Auca. The meat is juicy and quite tasty, reminding us of turkey or venison. The head is considered a particular delicacy and is usually reserved for the hunter.

<
Howler monkeys are the largest New World monkeys. They have a unique, amplifying resonance chamber with fine walls of bone in their grotesquely enlarged larynx. Their chorus in the early morning remains unforgettable: the males' hoarse metallic roaring penetrates kilometers through the jungle.

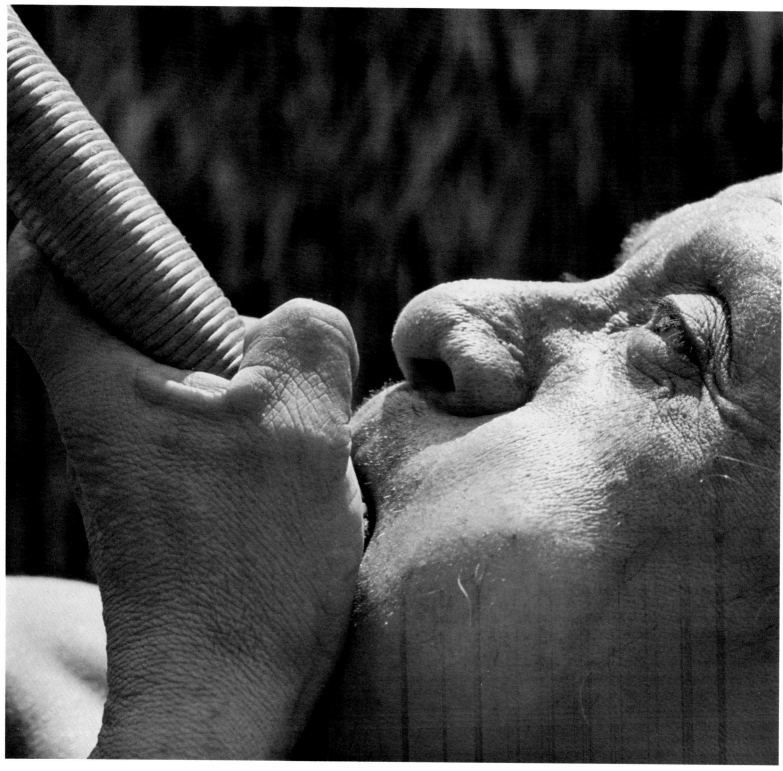

Good aim with the long heavy blowgun has to be learned. This silent weapon is superior to the gun for hunting birds and monkeys in the jungle.

> Caruae coating darts for his blowgun. He carefully dips the points in the boiled-up poison. By the fire the curare hardens into a shiny, lacquer-like coating. The darts are ready for the hunt.

Transfixed in amazement, Menga recognizes himself in the lens of the camera. At the same time his pupils reflect the double mirror-image of the photographer. Sparse beard, narrow eyes, broad flat nose, prominent cheek-bones, bright red spots of achiote paint and white balsa-wood earplugs lend his features the characteristic Auca stamp.

Caruae hunting >

Titae is the patriarch of his group. Two years earlier he had lost half of his people to the missionaries.

<
Auca spears! Symbols of a free people that has to fear for its independence. They have given the Auca the reputation of a savage, inaccessible tribe that 'hates all strangers and only lives to hunt and kill', a reputation that has spread far beyond their own borders.

Auca spears, made of extremely hard chonta-
wood, can measure up to three meters in
length. Their elaborate feather ornaments
underline the significance the Auca ascribe to
them as weapons for fighting and hunting.

Titae and Wenae help get Ana's baby safely across the muddy yellow Cononaco, swollen by rains.

The daily de-lousing ritual! In the late afternoon whole families often sit one close behind the other and pick the annoying pests out of each other's hair.

We are not about to give up. There must be a pilot and an airplane that can cope with the Cononaco runway. We receive a friendly but firm refusal from the Catholic mission of the Salesians: their Cessna is booked out for weeks ahead. No luck with the Protestants either. Bill Capp, head of the 'Alas de Socorro' MAF aviation group[4], has two Cessna-STOL Skywagons at his disposal, sturdy airplanes eminently suited for landing on short jungle runways. But one is being repaired and the other has no flights free in the foreseeable future. "Sorry, but why don't you try the army? Capitán Delgado has a Pilatus-Porter that can land on extremely short runways."

Delgado, our last chance, is in Quito till Sunday evening. Today is Thursday, but we are determined to wait. We spend the weekend at the Rio Napo and are back by Monday morning. But Delgado is nowhere to be found, and an audience with the Coronel is a cold shower. Impossible, his pilots have better things to do. "Muchas gracias, mi Coronel."

A final attempt: we try Bill Capp again and the miracle happens! Hearing our sad story he relents, checks his flight schedule once more and finds space for us on November 9. That is seventeen days off, but never mind! We have a pilot and a Cessna that can land on three hundred meters.

We spend the time in Cuzco and Machu-Picchu and are back in Quito on November 7. At the airport we are already greeted by the newspaper headlines: 'Auca on the Warpath' and 'Panic in the Jungle'. Over the weekend, news of new Auca attacks has reached the Ecuadorian capital: a five-man patrol from General Geophysical has been ambushed by the Auca and three 'Trocheros' have been killed. At the time of the attack, the patrol had been at the Rio Tivacuno, about sixty kilometers southeast of Coca. A second group of Trocheros had been besieged by Auca for several days in Camp Tiguino until they were rescued by an army helicopter. The episode was reported around the world. In our hometown, the Basler Zeitung reported on it under the headline 'Lances against Oil Prospectors':

"The 'Auca', an Indian tribe living in the Amazon jungle of northeastern Ecuador, have gone on the warpath to prevent whites from penetrating their territory. Three employees of a French prospecting firm who were looking for oil on behalf of the Ecuadorian government between the Coca and Napo rivers have been killed by the Indians. The 'Auca' ambushed the workers, who were cutting a path through the jungle, and killed them with three-meter-long spears. Two of the ambushed men could escape by jumping into the river and diving under the surface. They had to hide

4 Missionary Aviation Fellowship.

until the Indians stopped searching for them the next day. The 'Auca' laid siege to a company camp about thirty kilometers away with five workers in it for several days until an army helicopter came to their rescue.

The 'Auca' responded to their first contact with whites in 1956 by killing five North American missionaries – their 'discoverers'. Since then part of the tribe has settled down and gone over to wearing 'civilized clothing'. A group of these Indians has even applied for identification cards from the police in the provincial capital of Shiripuno recently. But a small part of the tribe has remained faithful to their nomadic life. The members of this group, which numbers about 300, live by fishing and hunting, wear no clothing and deform their ears with fist-sized wooden discs that are inserted into their earlobes. The Ecuadorian government has evacuated all whites from this tribal group's hunting grounds and has charged an army captain with the responsibility of making peaceful contact with the group. Oil prospecting is only to be continued after a peace treaty has been made."

The image of cruel, murderous savages, an image born of a combination of legend and fact, was once again nurtured by these bloody events. The local papers spoke of reprisals, of government protected concessions to drill for oil which were now jeopardized by a few Indios, of complex questions of Indian reservations but only rarely of the Auca's wish, much less their right, to protect their shrinking territory and their freedom by the use of weapons.

We beleaguer Sam with questions: What does he know about the ambush? Had the Cononaco group taken part? Do we have to give up our plans for good? We try to pinpoint the locale of the events on the map: barely seventy kilometers northwest of our destination on the Cononaco. But Sam is convinced that the attack was made by the Tageiri group, an aggressive, nomadic group of 30 or 40 Auca living north of the upper Cononaco in the Tivacuno and Tiputini river area. Invited by army leaders, Sam helps with the reconstruction of the ambush and tries to free the Cononaco group from suspicion. All flights over Auca territory have been forbidden except with special permission; and Sam is now particularly proud to be able to hand over a letter to us with instructions from the Chief of the General Staff, General Cabrera, for the commander of the Twentieth Bush Brigade in Pastaza to give us the necessary help and support for our forthcoming flight.

The military authorities in Shell-Mera are impressed by Cabrera's letter. Though they consider us totally mad, we have no trouble getting permission for our flight and are even guaranteed a Pilatus-Porter should our arrangements with Bill not work out. Bill has not been expecting us.

He greets us with "Don't you guys read the newspaper?" but is ready to keep his promise. "I'll leave you at the Cononaco and bring you back here, too. What happens in between is your business."

Next morning we are at the small MAF airport. Weather reports crackle from the short-wave radio next to the hangar. Tiwaeno and Villano report low blankets of cloud, and it is raining at the Curaray. But after lunch the weather is clear for take-off. We weigh ourselves and our luggage, taxi to the runway and a few minutes later Bill is flying the Cessna on an eastward course.

Bainca, who is about 12, is the first one to spontaneously discover a new form of representation. His hieroglyph-like symbols stand for caterpillars, beetles, leaves and trees.

An Island
in the Jungle

Once again we follow the sluggish brown serpentines of the Rio Villano. Black clouds threaten from the northeast. Not far past Camp Curaray, which we can still see glistening in the sun, we pierce a wall of grey and for long, anxious minutes we fly through heavy rain, which lashes loud and hard against the cockpit of our little Cessna. But then the sun begins shooting silver arrows through the fog. With the last drops of rain the sky seems to open wide and blue beneath us, and the vast, green sea of trees sparkles in the sunlight. We can see the Cononaco meandering in the distance.

For fifty kilometers we fly low over the winding river. And then suddenly the small ochre runway becomes visible through the trees. Bill throttles the engine and takes the Cessna further down in a wide arc for our first flight over. Hardly a hundred meters off the ground we can see yellow-brown figures running along the narrow path from the hut to the landing strip. Bill banks the plane and, only a few meters above the treetops, flies it parallel to the river towards the runway. A group of Auca is standing near the edge, gesticulating excitedly up at us. Further on crouches a man beating the ground with the palms of his hands, a gesture we interpret as an invitation to land.

But Bill pulls the plane up and once more the runway recedes into the distance again. We can no longer hide our excitement. Even our hard-boiled bush-pilot senses the tension: "Are you really sure you want me to land here?"

"Sure, Bill, let's go down!"

A final curve over the river and then we glide down between the trees lining the runway. The tires bump down hard twice, and then the Cessna taxis to a halt scarcely ten meters from the first Auca.

A throng of stark-naked Auca screaming excitedly – men, women and children – come crowding around the plane. Apprehensive but resolute, we climb out of the cabin and are immediately surrounded by naked bodies. Hands grasp at us and we are overwhelmed by a flood of loud, incomprehensible words. An Auca with pitch-black hair hanging down over his shoulders extends a bundle of long red macaw tail-feathers to us to show that we are being welcomed in peace.

In the meantime Bill has begun tossing our luggage out of the cabin. Before he returns to the controls, an Auca presses a feathered band to his forehead. As Bill leaves, he seems to be taking a whole world with him. We can hardly help feeling strangely uneasy as the red-and-white Cessna high above the trees becomes smaller and smaller, finally disappearing on the horizon.

But the Auca do not leave us much time to think. They crowd around us. Their hands are everywhere. We are touched, patted, smelled; they explore our bodies, unbuttoning our shirts and trying to unfasten our belts. They seem particularly intrigued by the hair on my chest; they stroke it and pull at it with cries of astonishment and delight. Their curiosity knows no bounds. More intimate parts of our bodies are not spared careful examination either; and a group of women and children seem to want to do an especially thorough job on Wally.

We do not offer any resistance. Sam has prepared us for all this, and we know we must not refuse. The Auca, who have for centuries had no contact with the outside world, consider themselves the only real and true people. They have only a very indistinct conception of the world of the strangers, the Cuwudi, which begins somewhere beyond the Rio Napo. In traditional Auca legends the Cuwudi appear as demons or cannibals, and traces of these beliefs have probably survived. Add to that the fact that the Auca are not familiar with clothing. Who knows what the strangers are hiding under it. Are they really people? Sam is convinced that the Auca would interpret a difference in or lack of genitals as an unmistakable sign of not being human. So their motivation is not merely curiosity; it is also the desire to determine just how human their rare visitors from another world are, thus protecting themselves from unpleasant surprises.

When they let up on us a bit, Sam becomes the centre of attention. They lay their arms round his shoulders and slap him on the back while besieging him with questions. He towers over all of them. Their speech is rapid and strikingly nasal. They are all talking at the same time, and Sam hardly has time to reply to one question before the next one is fired at him. But gradually the storm of excitement dies down, and then, as if it were the most natural thing on earth, they shoulder our equipment and lead us through the luxuriant undergrowth at the end of the runway. We balance our way over damp treetrunks lying across a clear rushing stream. Then the narrow, slippery path rises short and steep to the small clearing overlooking the river, where the large communal hut we had already noticed from the plane stands. Still as if in a dream, we stoop through the entrance and wait for our eyes to adjust to the semi-darkness. The air is cool and smoky, the floor of tamped-down earth dry and clean. Three fires smoulder beneath the ashes; next to them, light-colored logs, calabashes, and clay and metal pots. Above, a confusion of hammocks, plaited baskets, spears, blowguns and quivers. Two green parrots are doing acrobatics on a branch, and a frizzy woolly monkey is pulling at its lead, screaming blue murder. One corner of the hut is cleared for us, and we find enough space to sling our hammocks between supporting posts.

Some Auca help us to start a fire in front of the hut. As we prepare our first meal of rice and beans, they stand or squat around us, laughing and talking, observing our every movement and gesture with expressions of surprise and loud comments. A toppled treetrunk serves as a bench; and for the first time, over a cup of coffee, we have the time and the peace of mind to perceive this new and fascinating world with all our senses. And who would not be fascinated at the sight of these naked, light brown people. In the light of the setting sun they sit on their heels, flushed with excitement as they recount the arrival of their foreign visitors. Again and again their hands circle the earth like an airplane. They imitate the noise of the engine with low humming sounds. In between they slap their thighs in sheer delight and simply cannot bring themselves to end their chatter.

We cannot help thinking of all the well-meaning warnings about the 'wildest and most dangerous Indian tribe on earth'. These laughing, cheerful, primitive people, so childishly exuberant about our visit, who have welcomed us with such natural hospitality – can these be the unfeeling barbarians of the jungle, the feared, xenophobic spear-murderers? Maybe we are lucky and are encountering an exception. But it is much likelier that Sam's presence has smoothed the way for this friendly welcome.

Without him the undertaking would have been a rash adventure. As yet we know far too little about them, but we feel safe and secure among these natural, unspoilt people. We have a strange, scarcely describable feeling of contentment at being allowed to be with them. I cannot help thinking of Jean de Lery's remark: "I have found that I can trust these people whom we call 'savage' more and feel safer among them than among insincere, decadent people in many parts of France[1]."

Although the men are of small stature – barely taller than 1 m 50 cm – they have well-proportioned, strong bodies with muscular, sinewy arms and legs and strong broad feet with thick gnarled toes. They go completely naked apart from a hip-cord under which they tuck the foreskin of their penis. Their jet-black hair is cut in bangs just above the eyes and falls in strands over their broad shoulders. Their faces are hairless, although here and there a few short bristles may show above the upper lip

1 Brazilian Diary, 1556–1558.

The Auca find all the necessities of life in nature. Tender Chambira-palm leaf shoots provide the fibres which, after they are washed and dried in the shade, are rolled on the thighs to make coarse but strong yarn which they use for their skilfully knotted hammocks.

and on the chin. They have very little or no hair on their bodies. The women, who are about 10 cm shorter, are almost all broad-hipped, buxom and well-rounded without looking graceless. Parasites are probably the cause for their somewhat protruding stomachs. In contrast to the younger women, with swelling breasts and gleaming, taut skin, the older ones look worn-out, their skin dull and wrinkled, their breasts flat and sagging, having become prematurely slack through frequent pregnancies and lengthy periods of nursing. The women, too, wear nothing but the narrow, plaited, cotton hip-cord, which they call a 'kumi'. In comparison with the men, they have no pubic hair. Both sexes ornament their large, pierced earlobes with round, white, balsa-wood plugs, though we did see many with the holes in their earlobes stretched and empty. Broad flat noses, prominent cheekbones and narrow, almond-shaped eyes with a fold in the lid point to Mongolian origins.

The group is composed of four interrelated families. Three of them live together in the large hut, each family with its own area and hammocks around its fire. The fourth family lives alone in a hut situated a bit higher up. Sam introduces us to each of them in turn:

First there is Apa and his wife Camemo, with an infant cradled in a bark-cloth baby-sling. Next to them, Obi, one of their daughters, lively and well-built, with budding breasts and approaching the marriageable age, her younger sister Gewane and their two brothers Bainca and Tewae. Apa's bachelor brother Cincawae also lives with the family.

Then strong, friendly Menga and his wife Omamo, the oldest woman in the group, with their sons Nontowae, Menquere and Yata and their daughters Wadi and Waenonca.

Taciturn Caruae is next to be introduced. His two wives are Menga and Omamo's daughters. He has had three children with Ñawanae, the eldest a boy, Avancamo, and two girls, Watoca and Nonpo. Ñawanae is pregnant. When she walks she drags a deformed foot, the result of having been bitten by the feared bushmaster snake. Caruae and slant-eyed, full-bosomed Cacadi have not had any children yet.

Sturdy, short-haired Boca, who lives in the upper hut with his family, is Menga's son; his two wives are Apa's daughters. Boca and his second wife Awaenca are the only ones who wear worn-out, faded blue bathing trunks instead of the traditional kumi. Where can they have come from? When Sam translates our question, Boca only gives an embarrassed laugh but does not answer. He has had one daughter, Omatoqui, by Awaenca and another, little Gami, by his first wife Giicabae.

We watch Menga hollowing out the bore of a new blowgun. The two halves, which have been cut out of extremely hard Chonta-palm wood, will later be put together to make an oval pipe; it will be sealed with beeswax and wrapped with liana bark for a sure grip. In spite of the primitive tools used, the 10 millimeter bore is amazingly precise.

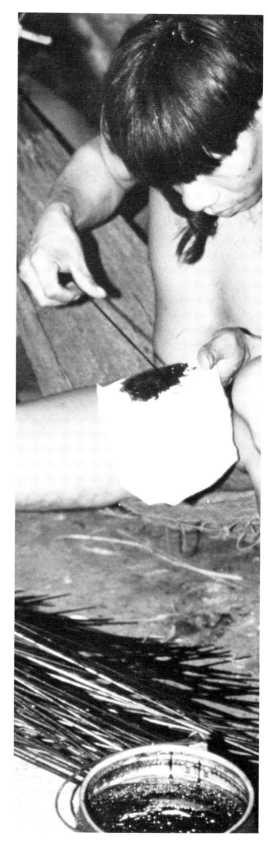

The Auca make no clear distinction between work and leisure. During a cosy chat, Ona renews his stock of blowgun-darts.

Cincawae coating the tips of his darts with curare.

A small tuft of kapok fluff is plied into a cuff at the blunt end of the dart, so as to seal the blowgun airtight. Then a sharp piranha tooth is used to cut a barb into the dart about 10 centimeters from the point, so that it will break should its victim try to pull the projectile out of its body before the curare has begun to take effect.

The shadows of the trees grow longer and darker. As the sun finally sinks into the forest, the Auca begin disappearing into the hut, and we too seek our hammocks. Rekindled fires flicker, and their restless light casts shadows of naked bodies. Half-asleep, a macaw makes grating noises. The woolly monkey, which has been roused in its corner, screams, and from one corner of the hut comes the heart-rending sigh of an owl. Only an arm's length from me Caruae climbs into Cacadi's hammock and makes himself luxuriously comfortable. He gives me a friendly smile and heartily breaks wind.

The Auca have no thoughts of sleep yet. The day has been too exciting for that; there are still many things to be gone into in detail. Even the children are wide awake. They can be heard giggling, whispering and laughing. And then they begin to sing: first one woman alone, in Auca falsetto, then another, until the men join in, unsteady and subdued at first and then in full, strong voice. A nasal and monotonous chant, but musical and captivating with its strange, rocking rhythm and long, recurring refrains.

As the fires gradually die, the voices begin to subside in the darkness; and soon the clear and distant 'Rrrrbit – Rrrrbit' of the frogs, the rustling and whispering of the mice in the roof and the piteous sighing of the small owl are the only sounds that break the silence.

In the pale twilight of the next morning Caruae slides out of his hammock, picks up a long blowgun, slings his quiver over his shoulder and disappears wordlessly through the back entrance of the hut. Now voices can be heard. A woman starts singing. There is loud, uninhibited farting on all sides: the Auca are greeting the new day! Apa crouches by the hearth, blowing into the smouldering embers, puts on some kindling wood, and fans the fire with a flat bundle of turkey tail-feathers until the flames rise. He passes a glowing log to Menga, who uses it to bring his own fire to life again. Women stretch and go to put pots on the fire. Natural urges drive people outside. The macaw croaks. The woolly monkey screams. The Auca household is awake.

Outside the air is cool and the ground damp. A fine veil of mist hangs over the river. The jungle stands placid and sleepy in the twilight of dawn. We enjoy a cup of hot coffee and are at peace with ourselves and the world.

Our morning wash provides the Auca with a proper show. The children as well as a few of the adults have followed us to the small stream and taken up their positions around us. They find everything we do new and

interesting, starting with the comic ritual of brushing our teeth. But the high point of the performance is unquestionably the magical conjuring trick with the white foam that comes out of that peculiar can and which that strange Cuwudi spreads on his face. Incredulous, almost afraid, they stare open-mouthed, their bodies frozen in amazement. But natural curiosity gains the upper hand. Boca is the first to grab at the miraculous foam with his pointy fingers. When he remains unharmed his tense face breaks into a broad smile. Now everyone wants to have some. Laughing and shouting, they spread lather on their faces, hair and bodies; our prosaic shaving-foam has given rise to a high-spirited new game.

Back at the hut the mood changes. Camemo brings me her baby, which is lying still and feverish in her arms: "Botimóti huaa quebi cuwudi!" – "Help me stranger!" – I manage to make out. But then, although Camemo speaks extremely slowly and clearly, for it is very important to her to be understood, Sam has to help. "My child is ill, make it well," he begins to translate. Her request places me in a dilemma; but after some initial hesitation, I decide that we really cannot deny her our help, modest though it may be. Camemo immediately realizes what I want her to do. Anxious not to spill any, she forces the calabash with an aspirin dissolved in water into the child's mouth and then puts it to her breast. A short time later Cincawae wants to have a nasty cut on his foot treated. Our medical knowledge is limited to basic first aid. Time is still needed for mutual understanding and trust to develop, and we cannot afford to make any mistakes now. We do not know the reason for the baby's high temperature. What would happen if the child died and we were considered responsible?

Although we are followed around faithfully wherever we go, particularly by the children, who do not want to lose sight of us for a moment, the Auca gradually seem to be getting back to their normal, daily routine. Omamo is working on a hammock. Auca hammocks, which take the women long, strenuous hours to make, are knotted out of Chambira-fibre yarn and are proof of their remarkable manual skills. The tender Chambira-palm[2] leaf-shoots provide the fibre, which is washed, dried in the shade and then rolled into coarse, strong yarn on the thighs. The hammocks are surprisingly comfortable and strong enough for two adults lying diagonally across from one another to sleep in. A husband may share his hammock with one of his wives or two sisters sleep in one, and very small children always sleep in one hammock with their mother.

2 Astrocaryum tucumá.

In some cases the yarn for the hammocks is partly dyed red; the dye is extracted from the bark and wood of the Wipita tree. The hammocks, their strands at both ends tightened around smoke-stained monkey bones, are stretched close to the floor and, being the only furnishings of the Auca house, are used for lying or sitting in during the day, too, so they are seldom seen folded and tied up.

Cincawae sits by the entrance of the hut, legs outstretched, whittling blowgun darts with a fragment of a machete. The ground around him is covered with shavings. The approximately 40-centimeter-long darts are cut out of the central rib of a palm leaf, and are worked until a regular, approximately two-millimeter-thick, elastic rod with a needle-fine point is left.

His brother Apa is squatting a few steps away, warming a pot of curare over the open fire. Using a piece of calabash, he skims off the blackish-brown skin that forms on the surface and carefully turns the points of the darts in the viscous mass until they are uniformly covered with poison. Skilfully he stacks up one dart after the other by the fire to dry. In an hour the curare has hardened into a shiny, lacquer-like coating. Now the darts are ready to be used for hunting; fifty or more are kept in a bamboo quiver, the opening covered by a lid made of bark sealed off with beeswax. A calabash ball filled with white kapok fluff dangles from it. Before shooting, the hunter pulls off a bit of kapok and plies it into a cuff at the blunt end of the dart so as to seal the blowgun airtight. The dart is notched about 10 centimeters from the point with the sharp teeth of a piranha-jawbone, so that it will break in case its victim, for instance a monkey, tries to pull the projectile out of its body before the curare has had time to penetrate into its bloodstream. While the Auca need not bother about their simple, easily made blowgun darts once they have been used, other Indians, who use bows and arrows, can hardly afford to lose their more sophisticated arrows.

Menga has decided to work on a new blowgun. The crudely cut halves are lying in front of the hut, and we can watch him hollowing out the bore with his broken-off knife blade. The hard, inflexible wood of the Chonta palm[3], with its completely straight, vertical grain, is a perfectly suited raw material. Chonta-wood is affected by neither heat nor humidity, so it never warps. Once the bore has been carved, the two halves are put together to make an oval pipe, sealed with black wax from a wild bees' nest and tightly wrapped with liana bark for a sure grip except for the mouthpiece, which is formed to suit the shape of the lips. The bore is

3 Guilelma Gasipaes.

then cleaned and polished with fine sand and water by patiently moving a long, thin, hard but very elastic rod of Chonta-wood through it until it runs absolutely straight through the blowgun. The precision of the ten-millimeter bore of the up to 2 m 80 cm-long pipe is astonishing, especially when one considers the primitive tools the Auca have at their disposal.

When fired horizontally, the blowgun's weight of about four kilos hardly allows steady aim. But the animals hunted with the weapon, mainly monkeys and birds, are almost all tree-dwellers, so before the weapon is fired it is placed in an almost vertical position with arms bent. But even so the hunter cannot afford to hesitate, for the gun's center of gravity leaves him only a few fleeting moments to aim.

Cincawae gives us a practical demonstration. He positions the blowgun with his muscular arms, distends his cheek-muscles and – swish! – the white-dotted dart is stuck high in a treetrunk twenty meters away. "Waaponi!" – Good, very good! – 'Waaponi' is an expression of happiness, satisfaction or unqualified agreement which we shall be hearing frequently. Smiling roguishly, he hands me the blowgun: "Now you try it, Cuwudi!" But my attempt is no more than a poor parody. The dart falls to the ground only a few meters from me, and I do not have to wait long for the Auca's mocking laughter.

The blowgun is used exclusively for hunting small to middle-sized animals. Larger mammals, especially the peccary, which is similar to the European wild boar, and even the puma or jaguar are hunted down with spears. These two- to three-meter-long lances, which are thrown or jabbed, are simple but perfect masterpieces of primitive technology. They, too, are cut from very hard Chonta-wood. The upper half is wrapped with lianas and often decorated with feathers. Three to six barbs are cut into both sides below the flat spear-point.

But it is not only for hunting that the spears lie handy in every hut. They also decide quarrels with enemy groups as well as personal vendettas within their own. In conjunction with the natural barrier of the rain forest, this feared weapon has so far remained an effective deterrent against unwelcome intruders. The spear has become a symbol of the independence and freedom of the Auca people. But it has also given them a reputation that has spread far beyond their own borders of being one of the most savage and dangerous Indian tribes on the South American continent.

When Caruae comes back from hunting, the sun is beating down mercilessly. He now returns to the hut as silently as he left in the early morning and drops his kill next to the fire: a fat woolly monkey, two capuchin monkeys, a toucan and a wild turkey. He has spent seven hours in the forest. Now he is tired and sits in his hammock waiting for Ñawanae to bring him a calabash full of chicha, which he drinks up greedily. Outside Cacadi begins plucking the birds. She puts the lovely, delicate breast feathers of the toucan aside; Caruae will decorate a headband with them later. In the meantime Ñawanae stirs the fire, puts new logs on and waits until there is a bright blaze. She then takes the woolly monkey and singes its hair over the fire. As the heat makes its muscles contract, it is as if one were seeing the monkey come to life and die again: its body distends to grotesque proportions, its legs swell, its hands close into fists, and its face, teeth bared, is distorted to a grimace. But Ñawanae is not impressed by this eerie sight. She turns the monkey in every direction until its hair has been uniformly burnt off and the skin is black, shiny and cracked. Then she cuts the meat into bloody, dark-red, fist-sized pieces and throws them into a large, black clay pot with peeled manioc-roots but no salt and lets it cook until tender. Monkey meat is juicy and quite tasty; it reminds us of turkey or venison. The head is considered to be a special delicacy and is reserved for the hunter. The toucan is roasted over the open fire and its scanty meat left to the children. Caruae offers us the turkey as a gift.

On the third day we have company! It is a second group of Auca, who live a one-and-a-half day's walk upriver on a tributary of the Cononaco. Their approach is noticed long before we can hear or see them, and now everyone is excitedly looking towards the opposite river bank. The Auca's hearing and vision are amazing. They can spot a bird or monkey high up in a tree where we see nothing but a profusion of green leaves, or sometimes minutes before our urban ears perceive the soft hum of an airplane flying high above us, they are already shouting, "Ebo, ebo!4" and pointing to the sky.

Tawny figures appear on the opposite bank. Silently they step out of the forest in small groups. First the men with spears and blowguns, then the children and women carrying heavy bundles on their tumplines. The river is about 35 meters wide and well over 2 meters deep in the middle. To cross it, they use an old cable left behind years ago by the runway builders and which now, fastened on either bank, sways permanently over the Cononaco. Moving hand over hand, they slide along the cable, carrying or dragging their weapons, quivers, baskets, hammocks and

4 Terms for things foreign to their culture are often borrowed from nature. Thus the word 'ebo' is used for both the wood bee and the airplane. 'Daegenemo' means dragon-fly and helicopter and 'apaika' means the moon and flashlight.

In late autumn the plum-sized fruit of the Mauritia palm brings some variety into the simple Auca menu. Baskets plaited on the spot out of palm leaves hang heavy and full from tumplines. Infants are never let out of sight; cradled in bark-cloth baby-slings, they are taken along everywhere.

Menga, the good genius of the Auca community, is always friendly and helpful. Without being asked to, he takes the heavy load of palm fruit from Cacadi's back.

<
Wadi has to get used to the fact that carrying heavy loads is usually left to women. She is carrying green bananas from a distant garden to the hut.

Compared with the luxurious and often spectacular ceremonial featherwork of some of the Indian tribes of Amazonia, Auca ornaments are modest. Menga's wife Omamo has woven pitch-black strands of his own hair into his arm bands made of jungle cotton. An Auca's 'kumi' is never missing. He feels naked without his hip-cord.

>
Boca lies on his stomach in his comfortable hammock and knots himself a new headband out of downy breast feathers.

Curare! Exotic, mystery-shrouded dart poison of the forest Indians. As early as the 16th century, Spanish padres brought news to Europe of the diabolical poison brewers who went naked, like wild animals. The Auca extract their paralyzing poison from the Strychnos liana. They coat their blowgun darts with the boiled-down, dark brown, viscous curare concentrate. By the fire the poison hardens into a shiny, lacquer-like coating which remains deadly for years.

The sawdust-like mass of scraped-off liana bark is pressed into a funnel of leaves and soaked with water until the poisonous substances start dissolving. After only a quarter of an hour the first drop of poison forms and falls into the calabash shell.

Again and again Menga spits a mouthful of water into the leaf funnel until the curare alkaloid starts to dissolve in the soaked mass.

Pottery is a dying art. Omamo, the oldest member of the group, has remained faithful to tradition. She coils the wall of the vessel out of slender ropes of clay. She smoothes the clay with a piece of calabash.

The Auca have a natural sense of cleanliness, and a refreshing bath in the river belongs to the daily routine. Little Wangi, who is only a week old, is still washed with water from a calabash shell and carefully examined for insects after every bath. Wangi died of a high fever at the age of two. When Camemo led us to her grave, her eyes filled with tears: "This is where we buried her. Her head is there, where the sun rises. That is where she came from and that is where she returned."

<
Apa tenderly brings his daughter Wangi in
out of the rain. Auca parents communicate
affection and a feeling of security to their
children through unconstrained body contact.

Awaenca has painted the traditional Auca
face mask with bright red achiote paint from
the top of her nose to just under her blue-
black hair.

Painting oneself with red 'caca' is very simple.
The fruit of the achiote bush, which
resembles a chestnut, provides the paint.
Once the shell of the fruit has been broken
open, all that needs to be done is to dip one's
finger into the creamy, colored seeds.

Their modest material culture can hardly be imagined without machete and steel axe anymore. With their earlier stone and Chonta-wood tools, clearing a new manioc garden could have taken months.

bags behind them through the water. Along with them, holding on for dear life, are macaws, parrots and a couple of black spider-monkeys. Small children are carefully taken across singly by their fathers and then left in their mother's care on the bank. It is a unique scene.

They climb the path to the plateau in single file, their naked bodies gleaming wet in the sunlight. They drop their bundles in front of the hut and come closer. The greeting ceremony follows age-old tradition: Titae, the oldest member of the group, speaks for all of them: "Pomonípa!" – We have come!

"Pomíni?" – Have you come? – answers Menga for his group.

"Pomonípa!" repeats Titae, and his people confirm this: "Éh, éh!" – That's right!

"Miníto pomíni waa abopa!" – Welcome!

"Eh, éh!"

"Waaquiwimi?" is the question now posed. – How are you?

"Waaquiwimopa!" – I'm fine!

That is all that is needed for the moment. No shaking of hands, no further gestures and no invitation to sit down. Nor is anything more expected. There is plenty of time left for gossiping and exchanging the latest news.

Titae, who has a drooping moustache and oriental goatee, is a widower; his wife died a few years ago after being bitten by a bushmaster snake. His eldest sons with their wives and children are with them: Tidicawae, who also has traces of a beard; Omanonqui, savage and sullen, with a mighty mane of hair; and Naenquiwi, who was born with six toes on each foot and six fingers on each hand. Then daughter Ana with an infant whose father is unknown, his unmarried daughters Wenae and Uruca and his sons Oña, Come and Namo. Pego, a bachelor with short hair and big gaps between his teeth, has joined the group, as have a young couple, the wife a girl of hardly sixteen with an infant in her baby-sling, her large, full breasts oozing large drops of milk that roll down her stomach.

How long will it take us to be able to tell them apart and call each one by his own name? Surnames are unknown, and we soon notice that the Auca do not pronounce their own names. If someone is called by the wrong name, he usually tolerates the faux-pas silently, and only the children's derisive laughter points out our mistake.

With obvious pride of possession, 'our' Auca veritably put us on display. Cincawae and Obi do the actual presenting. This time, too, we are examined down to the skin. A new attraction has by this time been discovered: my gold fillings. As though at a horse auction, Cincawae opens my mouth and shows the impressed guests the white stranger's teeth. The climax of it all is my wristwatch. My arm goes from ear to ear. First they listen long and attentively, then they break into broad smiles and imitate its 'tick, tick, tick, tick'. Waaponi! The function of a watch is beyond their grasp. They do not doubt that we wear such a thing only because we enjoy its ticking sound. The fact that it is 2.37 p.m. is meaningless to them. The indispensable, technical aids of a stress-plagued civilization become a parable of total irrelevance here.

Later a short heavy thunderstorm drives everyone into the hut. A few leaky spots are immediately mended: Omamo and Obi climb adroitly onto the supporting trunks and insert new green palm leaves into the transverse ribs of the roof. The room is full. With Titae's group, which will later settle into the two upper huts, there are exactly fifty Auca. They crowd around the entrance, rock in the hammocks, crouch on the floor, whittle, plait, gossip, sing and laugh. The macaws screech and the monkeys gibber. The rain patters on the palm-thatched roof, bright streaks of lightning flash, and thunder rolls somberly.

The rectangular communal house is roomy – eight by six meters – and solidly built. Closely set together layers of palm leaves are bent over the rafters into a compact, water-tight roof sloping from the four-meter-high ridge beam to the floor without lateral openings. The inner frame of young Chonta trunks is held together by lianas. The 80-centimeter-wide exit opens onto the clearing in the north, while a second, somewhat smaller, exit on the opposite side leads directly into the jungle. Not only are the hammocks attached to the supporting posts and struts; baskets, nets, quivers, sacks of kapok-fluff, bundles of Chambira-fibre, and bamboo cases for macaw feathers hang from them, too, with spears and blowguns lying prominently above.

Our tape recorder is a great success. The microphone is passed around; they speak their rapid monologues, their expressions serious, wait for the replay and listen raptly to their own voices. Sam helps us to translate. Cincawae's words will suffice as an example:

"I sleep and wake up. Now I am here. I am well here. We sit and laugh well. Titae and Tidicawae came across the river. They came well. Everyone came and we are glad. Now we are here. Apa went and hunted down a woolly monkey. We had meat and ate well. Tomorrow I am going hunting and will kill many, many spider-monkeys. There are too

Their ankles loosely bound together with a length of jungle vine, they nimbly climb the high, smooth trunks and fish the delicious fruit from the branches of Cecropia trees with long sticks.

Again and again women and girls bring home heavy nets bulging with palm-fruit.

many for us to eat. We smoke the meat. We have meat for many days. But now I am well here and am laughing."

Then Sam organizes the men into a large chorus. They crouch on the ground, crowded around the tape recorder, and sing about a peccary hunt until, after long repeated verses, the song comes abruptly to an end with the compulsory yodel. Waaponi!

The rain has been over for some time. Now, with the sun casting bright shafts of light into the semi-darkness, the Auca leave the hut, almost reluctantly, one by one. Half a dozen women and children go and dig manioc tubers out of the dark earth in the nearby garden. The field has been only superficially cleared, and the rotting trunks of felled trees lie about. In between, more than man-sized manioc plants grow close together. Their up to 30-centimeter-long, starchy root tubers are the most important calorie-providers in the jungle. They can be harvested all year round, and the modest plantation, which is not labour intensive, is important for guaranteeing the Auca nourishment and making them temporarily independent of successful hunts.

The women dig the brown tubers out of the ground with a machete, at the same time breaking new cuttings off the old stalk, placing them on the ground horizontally and covering them lightly with a thin layer of earth. In a little over half a year the plant will have grown tall again, and the tuber will be ready for harvesting. Peeled, cut into pieces and cooked in water until tender, manioc is the staple of the Auca diet. The Auca are only familiar with sweet, non-poisonous manioc, which they call 'canae' and which can even be eaten raw, though this is rarely done. The bitter manioc that occurs more often in South America would be highly dangerous if eaten raw. Its poisonous effect is caused by the prussic acid found chiefly in the milky juice of the tuber. The Indian tribes of South America have developed ingenious and often quite complicated methods of detoxification to make bitter manioc in various forms useful in human nutrition.

Manioc is also important in the production of chicha, a sweet, nutritious, milk-like drink, which the Auca, unlike other Indians, do not allow to ferment and become alcoholic. For its preparation, boiled pieces of tuber are mashed into a white pulp by hand or with a wooden paddle. As a woman stirs the mash, she takes mouthfuls of it, chews them thoroughly and spits them back into the pot. Through this, to us not very appetizing, process the enzymes in her saliva hasten the slight fermentation of the chicha. Before the pulp becomes alcoholic, however,

it is diluted with water and drunk on the very next or even the same day.
A few banana trees are scattered at the edge of the clearing, but they do
not yet bear fruit. The green bananas that hang in the Auca's huts to
ripen come from the old garden near the place they used to live. Maize,
sweet potatoes, pepper, beans, sugar cane, rice, peanuts and papayas are
still unknown here; so is tobacco, which is otherwise seldom missing
among Indians. Chonta palms, calabash trees, achiote bushes and cotton
grow wild.

Thus the Auca's menu is extremely simple and monotonous as well as
being unsalted and unspiced; and it is easy to understand the importance of the meat brought in by the hunters. During our stay, apart from
occasional bananas and a very few wild berries or orange naranjillas, it
is the reddish, plum-sized, pine-cone-like fruit of the Mauritia palm,
which they call nontoca, that brings a bit of variety into their diets.
Again and again we see women, their backs bent beneath their burden,
carrying bulging nets and baskets full of nontocas home on their tumplines. The meagre fruit pulp that surrounds the stone is boiled in water
and gets a floury consistency and a sweet-and-sour, lemon-like taste.
Nontocas yield a nutritious and refreshing drink. In spring it is the red
fruit of the Chonta palm that is particularly appreciated. The time
when the Chonta fruit is ripe and the 'monkeys are fat' is the best time
of year for the Auca, and they celebrate its advent with singing and a lot
of chicha made of manioc and ripe bananas.

In the late afternoon, as the fiery rays of the sun begin to lose their
strength, the Auca sit in front of the hut chatting and picking annoying
insects out of one another's hair. Often three or four crouch one behind
the other, adeptly pushing the hair of the person in front to all sides and
examining his scalp carefully for irritating parasites. The lice that are
discovered are picked out with thumb and forefinger and then cracked
with the incisors. It would be going too far to attribute ritual significance to the profane activity of de-lousing, but even if it is nothing more
than a necessary part of daily hygiene, we feel it to be, almost involun-
tarily, a symbolic expression of belonging together.

Camemo is glad that her little daughter Bogenai is healthy again, and
she has not forgotten the help we gave her. She strokes my shoulder and
says: "Waakae bitapa!" – You did that well! – and then places the tiny
infant trustingly into Wally's arms.

Children are at play. Awancamo and Tewae have tied fine, Chambira
fibres around the hindlegs of a pair of fat furry bumblebees and are

Before the monkeys, cut up into fist-sized pieces, are put into the cooking pot, their hair is singed over an open fire.

whirring them around their heads like little toy airplanes. Bainca is hunting butterflies and lizards with a boy-sized blowgun. Half a dozen boys and girls are frolicking on a steep slope and sliding down an improvised slide of wet mud on their stomachs.

The men are sitting together whittling darts, talking about hunting, cracking jokes and teasing each other with innuendoes that are clearly sexual in nature. Apa elaborates today's hunting experience with a wealth of details. With animated eloquence he relates how he managed to shoot five squirrels out of a tree one after the other because in the ecstasy of copulating with a female they had discovered, they were so eager not to miss their turns that they did not notice the hunter. "What a way to go!" remarks Sam, and now the women join in the men's laughter.

It is the loveliest time of the day. On the way back to their sleeping trees pairs of scarlet macaws soar noisily over the clearing. A toucan circles low and lands on the branch of a nearby tree, and a snow-white heron glides silently across the river, takes off and flies into the purple disc of the setting sun.

Twilight brings the first fireflies, and a pair of night-hawks flit low above the ground with their clear 'tschiiiu-tschiiiu'. A moonless, tropical night falls on the forest like a velvet blanket sparkling with stars. The loud call of an owl close by breaks through the chorus of cicadas and frogs, and the reply is like a distant echo in the dark: "Wuuu-uhu-uhu." We snuggle in our hammocks in the warm, flickering light of the glowing fire; and once again it takes the Auca quite some time until they have talked and sung themselves to sleep.

Next morning Menga and Tidicawae want to stock up on curare for their group. We have heard and read so much about this mysterious, exotic dart poison used by South American Indians and never imagined that we would someday be allowed to watch it being produced.

As early as the 16th century, Spanish padres, the Conquistadors' zealous chroniclers, brought news to Europe of diabolical poison brewers, "who went naked as the wild animals and could hardly be distinguished from them." With admirable imagination they testified to the gruesome effects of curare and impressed astonished believers with descriptions of how it was made:

"They boil poisonous snakes, great black ants, many scorpions, poisonous worms and revolting spiders in a pot of water and wait until, in their agony, the dying animals discharge their poisons."

Or:

"They hang toads over the pot and beat them with switches until the toads' poisonous sweat streams down[5]."

The reports started becoming more realistic with Alexander von Humboldt, who was able to observe curare being made on the Orinoco in the early 19th century. 100 years later, modern research on the legend-surrounded poison began. In 1935 the active ingredient of curare was isolated in cristalline form, and in 1958 the first synthesis was achieved of Toxiferin, one of the most effective substances in curare, which is used in present-day pharmacology for the production of indispensable muscle-relaxants.

It is the paralyzing poison extracted from the Strychnos liana[6] that makes the blowgun loaded with darts an effective hunting weapon. Curare is only effective once it has entered the bloodstream, and thus the meat of the animal that has been killed remains edible. The poison spreads rapidly through the bloodstream, paralyzing its victim's muscles, including its respiratory organs; death is caused by suffocation.

The effect of the poison is dependent on the size and weight of the animal. Small birds fall out of trees within seconds like ripe fruit. Twenty-pound howler monkeys often sway on branches for minutes until, as they become increasingly paralyzed, they lose their grip and crash to the ground through the maze of leaves. The blowgun's great advantage is that it is so noiseless a weapon. When an experienced, light-footed hunter silently stalks a horde of monkeys, he can often kill three or four of them before the rest become aware of the danger, particularly as the monkey's instinct is to expect a threat from above, from its deadly enemy the harpy eagle.

Menga has lugged light-green Strychnos lianas, some as thick as a human arm, from the forest. He and Tidicawae use machete fragments to scrape the bark and top layer of wood onto spread out palm leaves. When the pile is large enough, Tidicawae very carefully begins to press the shavings into the leaves, and Menga helps him to bind them into a funnel with strips of bast. He hangs the funnel between two spears rammed into the ground at an angle and places a calabash shell under it. Now they take turns filling their mouths with water from a second calabash and spitting small amounts into the funnel. The water filters slowly through the softening mass to the bottom opening, dissolving the poison in the process. After about fifteen minutes the first drop forms and falls into the calabash. Two hours later the operation is over and the

Menga and Tidicawae renewing the group's supply of curare. They scrape the bark of the Strychnos liana onto palm leaves with fragments of a machete.

Tidicawae carefully presses the sawdust-like mass into the leaves ...

5 In fact the Chocó Indians of Colombia coat their blowgun-darts with the extremely poisonous skin secretion of a small tree frog.
6 Strychnos toxifera.

... and Menga helps him to wrap them into a funnel with strips of bast.

They hang the leaf funnel between two spears rammed into the ground at an angle and stand the calabash shell underneath. Then they take turns taking mouthfuls of water from another calabash and spitting small amounts into the funnel again and again. As the mass begins to get soaked, the water slowly seeps to the bottom opening, dissolving the poisonous substances. After fifteen minutes the first drop has formed at the bottom of the funnel and fallen into the shell. Two hours later the process is completed and the calabash is full of a clear liquid which will later be concentrated into viscous, blackish-brown curare over the fire.

bowl is full of a clear liquid that will be concentrated later into blackish-brown, viscous curare over the fire.

According to the Linguists' documents and other sources, there are supposed to be certain rituals and tabus concerning curare production. Thus it is claimed that women are not to show themselves in the vicinity during the operation, and the hunter is said to be forbidden to drink chicha or eat fish because this would dilute the poison. But we ourselves could see absolutely no ritual regulation of the task.

It does not take the Auca long to notice that my curiosity knows no bounds. They call me when a hunter has returned with a pair of fat, heavy howler monkeys; when pairs of fresh-water porpoises come up the river and jump out of the water at regular intervals, diving gracefully below the surface again; or when a bushmaster is coiled in the grass on the river bank, hissing and dangerous, ready to strike and nearly proving fatal to Wadi in the evening twilight. They bring us lizards, small, brilliantly-colored tree-frogs, turtles, praying mantes, bizarre beetles and many insects we are not familiar with, scorpions, tarantulas and palm-sized, iridescent-blue morpho butterflies. Today Pego has seen a huge anaconda at the edge of a pond, but by the time he gets us to the spot with our cameras ready, all that is left is a broad track leading through the grass into the muddy water. But then they ferret an almost two-meter-long fer-de-lance serpent out of the bushes. Using a forked branch, Pego manages to pin the snake to the ground and then quickly grasps it behind the head. Once he has broken out its poisonous fangs with his machete, it becomes a toy for the children. They throw stones at it and tease it mercilessly until it attacks and is finally allowed to escape into the underbrush again.

In the burning sun, sweat streams from every pore and attracts small, black, stinging gnats and wasps. The bites of these pests leave behind itching, painful swellings that later remain visible on the skin as small black dots. The big cats and snakes are not one's worst enemy in the jungle. It is the myriads of creeping, crawling, flying tormentors of the insect world that can so quickly and mercilessly destroy the idyllic mystique of the jungle. Luckily there are few mosquitoes here. But those damned chiggers! They are parasitic, microscopic, red ticks picked up while walking through the grass. They climb up one's legs and burrow into the skin, with a distinct preference for the warmer regions of the body. They only make themselves noticeable later through almost intolerable itching and tiny swellings on the skin. Insect repellents are of

no use at all. What would we do without our Auca! Every day they examine us for chiggers digging them out with a palm-thorn and freeing us of our torment. Ants can leave behind bad bites, too. The bite of the three-centimeter-long conga ant is particulary feared. Leafcutter ants, which walk in columns carrying pieces of leaves that look like green sails back to their subterranean burrows, never bothered us. Much more dangerous are the huge instinct-driven columns of tiny, voracious, army ants, which, protected by their soldiers, attack anything they come across. The Auca, whom we only rarely see perspiring, take the insect plague with greater equanimity. Nonetheless, their skin is also covered with black dots, and chiggers sometimes irritate them, too. When they return from the hunt, we can observe again and again how without being asked an elder daughter will examine her father for ticks.

Boca, too, has decided to avoid the heat. He is lying in his hammock working on a feather diadem. Downy red, yellow and white feathers glisten all over the floor in front of him. He selects his colors carefully and attaches the feathers close together, one after the other, to a narrow, flexible, wooden hoop. Obviously satisfied with the result, he finally presses the feathered wreath to his forehead. Waaponi! Particularly beautiful headbands have pure white heron feathers or long, red and blue macaw tail feathers; and once we saw one with a magnificent bunch of soft, greyish-black harpy-eagle feathers.

A few days ago we were allowed to watch indefatigable Menga helping his wife Omamo to plait armbands. Horizontal sticks attached with Chambira yarn to two spears stuck in the ground form a simple but functional plaiting frame. Omamo wove pitch-black hairs, which she cut off Menga's head with a sharp blade whenever she needed one (!), into the warp of the tautly stretched cotton threads. Lustrous red toucan feathers bundled around a thin stick of wood with black beeswax completed this unique arm ornament. I was speechless when Menga tied the bands round my upper arm as a gift. How could I repay this expression of friendship?

To make the black clay pots, which are unfortunately being replaced by metal pots, Omamo uses the coil method, gradually building up the walls of the vessel with slender cords of well-kneaded clay.

Compared with the luxurious and often spectacular ceremonial feather-work of many of the Indian tribes of Amazonia, the Auca's feather ornaments and body painting are rather simple. It may be characteristic of their way of life that carving, painting and artistic decoration of ceremonial and functional objects are lacking. As nomadic hunters and gatherers with undemanding manioc gardens, they own nothing that is not absolutely necessary and cannot be carried from one dwelling place

In the late afternoon, blood-smeared hunters return to the clearing with black, stiff-bristled peccaries heavy on their tumplines.

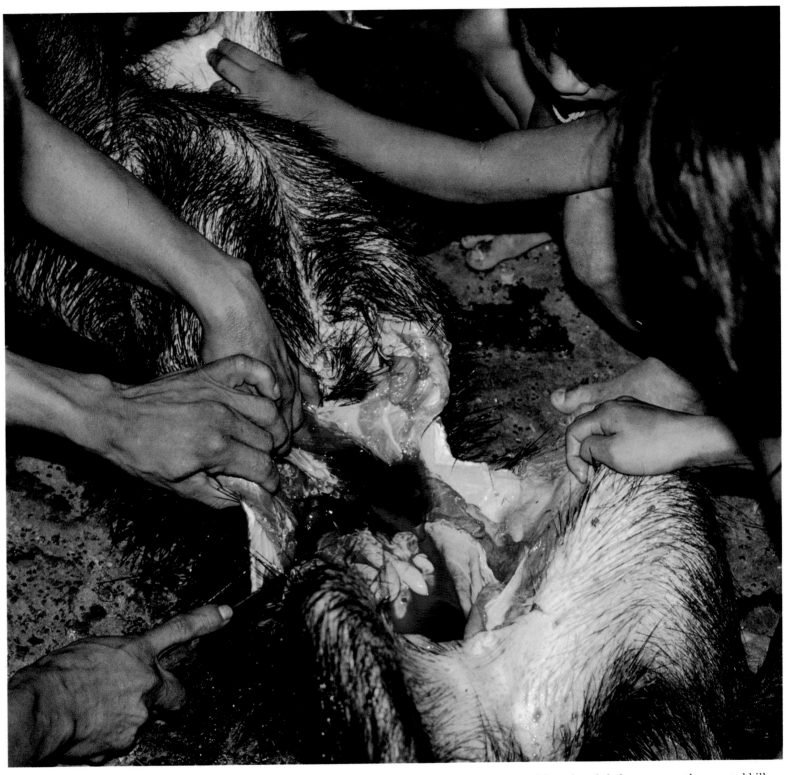

Many hands help to cut up the coveted kill. Every hunter dreams of a herd of peccaries, of plenty of meat and the delicious aroma of ham being smoked slowly over the fire.

<
Menga and Omamo singe the bristles of a peccary over the open fire.

Menga expertly cuts up his kill. Some of the
peccary meat will be boiled in water until
tender, the rest smoked over the fire so that it
can be kept for several days.

>
A little Auca girl gilded by the last rays of the
sun. The hunters had cut the baby peccary
out of its mother's womb.

They still have time to be idle! The scorching afternoon heat drives the Auca into the cool shade of the hut. They rock in their comfortable hammocks, perfectly willing to spend some time relaxing and talking. Free from material worries, they possess the enviable ability to enjoy the present with genuine animal contentment.

At the age of about 12, Wadi is fully aware of her future role. Even before reaching sexual maturity, Auca girls gradually begin to take part in all the duties of daily life. They fetch water from the stream, get firewood, pluck birds, peel manioc, help take care of their younger brothers and sisters, learn to plait and to do everything else that will be expected of them as married women one day.

The living, trussed-up, long-haired bundle at the end of Menga's blowgun has turned out to be a two-toed sloth. It is probably the strangest creature living in the tropical treetops. It hangs upside-down from the branches by its two, long, sickle-like claws. It is a master of camouflage. The greenish tint of its shaggy coat is caused by microscopic algae that flourish there. It needs a jungle hunter's keen sense and good eyes to spot a sloth high in the profusion of green leaves. The Auca do not particularly like its meat. Menga's reason for catching this sloth was to surprise his white guests from beyond the Rio Napo.

Hunting is the focal point of their lives. Seven
hours have passed since Menga reached for
his blowgun in the first pale light of dawn.
Proud and enthusiastic, he relates all the
details of the hunt, complete with sound
effects. The young howler monkey has survived the fall from high up in a tree clutching
its mother's fur. Its heart-rending sobs only
abate when Giicawae puts it to her breast to
nurse. The Auca keep it as a pet and give it a
new home. But the magnificent macaw ends
up in the pot.

In spite of the loving care it had received, this woolly monkey was found dead at the end of its lead one morning. It did not end up in the pot though; Wadi took it quietly to the forest and buried it there.

No hut lacks captive wild animals. Apart from monkeys, the Auca zoo mainly includes birds like macaws, parrots, falcons and owls. Young parrots are fed manioc gruel directly from their keepers' mouths, and small monkeys share their foster-mother's milk with nursing infants.

The camera catches Obi, who is usually mischievous and full of fun, at a pensive moment. She is about 14 and is thus of marriageable age. But she will have to wait! Nontowae, her eldest cousin, is only 11 and will not be thinking of marriage for a long time to come. Through the Linguists' untiring missionary efforts, the free Auca groups have shrunk considerably, and finding a partner has become a problem for Obi.

to the next without much trouble. Neither the attraction of amassing unnecessary belongings nor the artistic impulse exists. Specialization, including artistic fields, develops only once agriculture and the breeding of domestic animals have made a society dependent on and thus tied to one place.

Their feather work and necklaces of jaguar or peccary teeth and puma claws are mainly the trophies and amulets of successful hunters. They may be considered expressions of creative art to only a limited extent and are in no way an indication of rank or honour. Furs and skins are used neither as ornaments nor as functional objects. Women, distinguishing themselves clearly according to their duties, never ornament themselves with feathers, teeth or claws of animals. They do, however, wear the actual tribal symbol, the balsa-wood earplug.

Body painting with luminous red 'caca' is also very simple. The paint comes from the chestnut-like fruit of the achiote bush[7]. Once the shell of the fruit has been broken open, all that need be done is to dip one's finger into the greasy, colored seeds. While men paint only a few dots and lines on the upper part of their faces, women and girls draw a broad red band all across their faces from the tip of the nose upwards to the eyebrows and sometimes broad stripes along the calf from ankle to below the knee.

The hip-cord, or kumi, which men use to tie their penises up to protect them against dirt, thorns and insects, does not seem to serve a particular purpose for the women. It does, however, have more than purely decorative significance and should be interpreted as symbolic clothing. The Auca have their own sense of modesty and their own etiquette regarding their nakedness. Without their kumi they do not feel 'dressed', and they do not take it off even to bathe in the river. Women seem to learn very early to keep their knees together when they crouch so as not to expose their vulva unnecessarily. We never saw them sit or lie in their hammocks with legs spread either.

We watch Omamo making one of the increasingly rare, large, black, clay pots. She kneads a lump of clay to the proper consistency and rolls it on the ground into long, slender ropes, using the coil technique to build up the wall of the vessel. Now and then she inserts a glowing piece of wood in the growing vessel to help set the clay. As she presses the clay spirals together with her fingers, we are amazed to see the first symmetrical, if only rudimentary, ornament being created. But Omamo sees it differently; with a calabash scraper, she smoothes the walls flat again

7 Bixa orellana. For some time now, the dye has been exported to Europe and used as a basis for producing lipstick.

so that they are as they must be and have always been. So much for art! Music is another neglected muse. Musical instruments, be they simple drums or flutes, do not exist among the Auca. The only thing that comes close enough to be called a musical instrument is a bamboo tube, which they use for their dances during the chonta harvest festivities or on other special occasions; but no more than a single sound can be produced on it. It is often the same bamboo tube that serves to store their beautiful macaw tail feathers.

Like a kaleidoscope continually creating new patterns out of coloured pieces of glass, life in the little clearing brings new images and impressions daily, and our last morning comes much too soon. It has been pouring almost all night, and now rain is still dripping from the trees and the sky is dark and gloomy. Bill should be coming today, but we can hardly imagine him making it in this terrible weather. The general mood is not too good either. The ground in front of the hut is muddy and dirty yellow, and our cold, clammy clothes stick to our skin. The Auca are sitting around sullenly. Their general waterfall of words is reduced to a few gruff remarks. For the first time we hear children crying.

At four o'clock there is sudden excitement. With cries of "Ebo-ebo-ebo!" they all run outside the hut as if chased by demons. More than a minute passes, and then we, too, can distinguish the hum of an engine above the rushing noise of the rising river. Then we recognize the outlines of a Cessna breaking through a hole in the fog, banking just above the treetops towards the river and coming in for a landing. The plane touches down on the puddle-covered runway spraying fountains of water left and right and skids to a halt at the end of it.

Now every minute counts, for if the weather changes again, the Cessna will not be able to take off. We hastily pack up what is left, and then everyone helps us down the slippery path with our luggage. The little stream has swollen to a brownish-yellow torrent, and we have some trouble crossing the slippery treetrunks to the runway. Bill is ready to start. Our words of farewell stick in our throats.

"Gomonípa!" ... We are leaving! Waaponi, Huaorani, Waaponi!

The wheels dig deep into the soaked ground under the new weight, but when Bill shoots through the splashing puddles with full power, the Cessna takes off surprisingly easily. For a few seconds we see the Auca standing at the edge of the runway through our mud-spattered windows.

Then we are above the forest and the fog that lies over the trees like the smoke of a thousand hearths. Finding ourselves back in our own reality again is like waking up from a dream, and the world of the small Auca clearing on the Cononaco is swallowed up by the jungle again.

Manioc garden. The root tubers of the more than man-sized bushes are the most important calorie-providers in the Auca jungle.

Boca's sketch of an Auca hut is astonishing. He has drawn its inner Chonta-wood frame from above. To show the hammocks, he has 'uncovered' part of the roof! A trail leads from the hut to the forest, which he has populated with monkeys, a deer and, at the bottom right, an anteater.

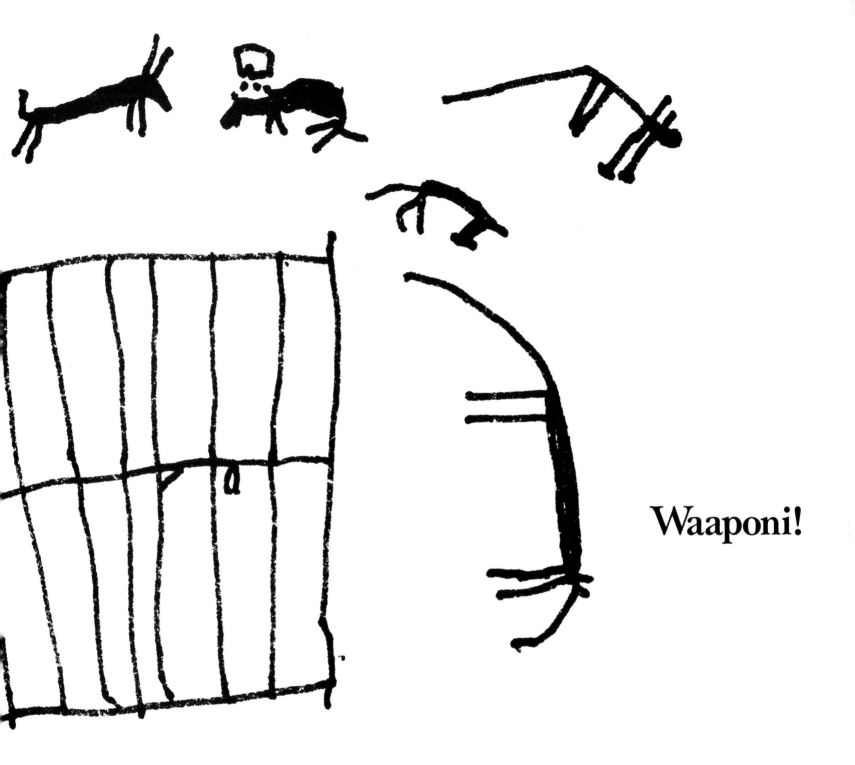

Waaponi!

When we climb out of the cabin of the Cessna at the Cononaco a year later, there are only women and children there to greet us. Omamo is burning with a high fever. It is an effort for her to stand; and she looks to Wally for help and clings to her, moaning. A few of the children are feverish, too. Where are the men? And where are Cacadi, Obi, Wadi, Bainca and Nontowae?

The sun is high in the deep blue, cloudless sky, and above the clearing the air shimmers in the heat. Sam, Boca and Cincawae have built us a new hut on a flat, slightly elevated spot only a few meters from where the bank slopes steeply down to the river. Entering the hut, I ram my head into a sharp, horizontal beam hidden by palm leaves. I am still dazed, and as I look for malaria pills and aspirin for Omamo and the children, the sweat runs into my eyes and blood trickles down from my forehead to my chin, falling to the ground in bright red drops. This is not the reception we had imagined!

We have the hut to ourselves. It is roomy, with a long platform of split bamboo for our sacks, food and cameras, a treetrunk as a bench and the luxury of a low table made of wooden planks hewn with a machete. Young avocado and lemon trees grow around the hut, and here and there banana trees grow, their fruit still small and green. We shoo away a few reddish-brown, fist-sized tarantulas which had retreated from the hot sun into the cool shade of the hut, hang up our hammocks and feel at home again.

Shortly after four o'clock the Cessna is back with three hundred kilos of rice, two sacks of corn and raw peanuts for the Auca, a second flight having been unavoidable because of the weight. At first I had been openly sceptical at Sam's suggestion. The corn and peanuts, intended as new seed, seemed all right to me, but I feared that the gift of rice might ultimately lead to an undesirable condition of dependence. But Sam's arguments were sound: after our first visit, Titae's group had decided on a new dwelling-place upriver, but had lost half of its people to the Linguists shortly afterwards. With their usual promises, the missionaries had managed to tempt three young families and our friend Pego from the group and had taken them to the Tiwaeno Reservation by helicopter. In the meantime, using his contacts with the military government, Sam had been successful in having the Linguists denied landing permission on the Cononaco runway. Now he wants to try to convince Titae and the rest of his people to return to the Cononaco, for he believes that they are better protected from the missionaries there[1]. All the members

With loud cries of 'Urä, urä!', their spears shouldered, the hunters disappear into the forest.

1 When we visited them recently with our old globetrotter friends, Ted and Nelly Birkhäuser, we found Titae's group at the Cononaco again. There was plenty of manioc, and though the Auca group had grown to 44, there still seemed to be enough game to hunt. Naenquiwi and Gami with little Oma were there again, happy though an illusion poorer. Sam had managed to bring them back from the Reservation.

The fact that Apa has left the whole front of his new hut open shows how safe he and his family feel from surprise attacks by hostile groups here at the Cononaco.

of Menga's group are still living on the Cononaco and evidently have nothing against Sam's attempts at patronage. Their problem is the manioc supply. The yield of their original plantation is no longer sufficient, and tubers from the new garden they have cleared in the forest should be left until they have ripened to full size. Until that time, our rice is meant to help bridge the food gap.

In the meantime, the men's absence has been explained. This morning Cacadi had brought news of a large herd of wild boars. She was on her way home from the garden near their old home, where the huts are now rotting, her carrying bag hanging heavy with green bananas from her tumpline. Suddenly she was confronted with the vanguard of a dark mass of grunting, snorting white-lipped peccaries. She immediately dropped her burden and ran home as fast as her legs could carry her, shouting, "Urä, urä, urä!"

In the Auca community, life depends on the hunt. A good hunt means meat and contentment. The hunter dreams of a herd of peccaries, of an abundance of meat, of the aroma of ham being smoked slowly over the fire. But peccaries cannot be found very often, and when Cacadi's excited cries rang across the river from afar, the men grabbed their spears and ran wildly down the path, crossed the river and disappeared into the forest with Obi, Wadi, Bainca and Nontowae behind them.

Now, in the golden light of the setting sun, they return, pull themselves along the cable across the river, climb up the steep bank to our hut with the black, stiff-bristled, trussed up animals slung over their blood-smeared shoulders, and drop their heavy burden in the grass.

They are happy to see us again. There is general back-slapping all round and many laughing "Waaponi!". They have remained the same! – healthy, muscular, sinewy, the warm brown skin of their naked bodies wet, taut and gleaming; their hair as black as ebony. Boca is still in his faded blue shorts. All of them are in the best of moods, for they have had a successful hunt: a huge wild boar, two sows and a baby cut out of its mother's body. Cincawae relives the hunt for us: he points to invisible animals, rocks the spear in his hand, then whips it back with a sudden, flowing movement, rises to his toes and with concentrated energy, the tendons of his arms as taut as ropes, throws the weapon with a shrill cry and lets it crash to the ground. We hear the grunting and the snorting and the chattering of the peccaries' teeth, and the bright 'Waw-wae-wae' of the young wild boars. We hear the spears hitting their targets, and again and again the frantic cries of the hunters. Apa, Menga, Boca and

Caruae confirm Cincawae's report with exclamations of: "Eh, éh, éh!" – Yes, that's how it was! That's how we killed them! Waaponi!

They had arrived at the spot where Cacadi had seen the herd and followed their clear tracks in the churned-up earth through the trampled underbrush until the noise of the peccaries was in front of them like the dull thunder of a distant storm[2]. "How large was the herd?" "Nangi, nangi, nangi!" Lots of them! Seven times Cincawae spreads the fingers of both hands towards us: seventy! In contrast to the small groups of roaming collared peccaries, which will try to face down any attacker with a show of great chattering of teeth and bristling neck hair and will even risk fighting with a jaguar, white-lipped peccaries immediately flee, leaving the hunter very little time to bag a few of the escaping herd.

Silently they had stalked the herd against the wind, staying in contact with one another only by whistling. They got closer and closer to the flank of the herd until the large, black, leader boar, scenting danger, came crashing out of the underbrush nearly running Boca down. But Boca managed to jump to one side and with a piercing shriek rammed the spear into the animal's side. Now everyone began attacking the panicking animals. With loud cries, they let their spears fly; and before the peccaries, which were scattering in all directions, could flee deeper into the forest, two more animals fell victim to spears. A fourth was wounded and left behind a track of blood through the forest, but the hunters followed it in vain.

When Cincawae comes to the end of his lively description of the hunt, the promise of fresh meat drives them to their huts and they leave us alone by the river. We sit in candlelight over a well-meaning attempt at Irish coffee, listening to the chorus of cicadas and frogs and allowing ourselves to be possessed by this wonderful, uncomplicated world.

In the early morning, limbs and thoughts still stiff with sleep, I am drawn out of the hut by a chorus of howler monkeys. Their hoarse sounds, somewhere between roaring and barking, comes from the distance. The first rays of the sun are breaking through the veil of fog, making the dewdrops gleam in the grass. A wild duck, its wings whirring, flies low over the water, and somewhere nearby a few noisy chachalaca hens are chattering 'guacharáca-guacharáca'. Menga, Boca and Cincawae come down the path from the upper hut followed by Obi with a few children. They come bearing gifts: a beautiful, scarlet macaw and a chambira necklace with puma claws and peccary tusks. They make themselves comfortable in our hammocks, ask for pocket-knives, look

Menga makes a fire in the ancient way of his ancestors, by twirling a piece of wood.

2 Sometime later, as we were waiting for the men to return from a peccary hunt, we heard thunder in the distance. Titae and a group of women sitting with us immediately began excitedly shouting, 'Urä-urä!'. They were totally convinced that the hunters had just speared the leader of the herd, and that the rest of the animals were now scattering in all directions. (In 'Nomads of the Long Bow', Allan Holmberg relates that the Siriono of eastern Bolivia associate thunder with the sound of peccaries falling to the ground.)

The razor-sharp, triangular teeth of the piranha can be a real danger. These notorious, predatory fish can be found in most of Amazonia's waters. A school of piranha can devour a large mammal down to the bone in only a few minutes. But their proverbial voracity seems to be dependent on several complex factors and to differ from type to type. The Auca disregard the danger. We followed their example and enjoyed our daily bath in the river with no misgivings.

<
As long as there is enough monkey meat, the Auca only fish to pass the time. Boca has decided to try one of the steel hooks and fishing lines we have brought along at a nearby lake.

Boa constrictor. Giant snakes and forest demons are best left alone! If someone kills a boa or an anaconda, he must subject himself to a strict ritual, otherwise small snakes will grow in his stomach and he will die. But anacondas over 10 meters long belong to the realm of myth and legend. Even if they are not encountered often, poisonous snakes constitute a constant danger for the Auca. On the Cononaco it is mainly the large bush-master whose enormous fangs can mean disaster. Menga's father and Titae's wife were both killed by the bite of a bushmaster. Ñawanae drags a badly deformed foot when she walks as a consequence of having been bitten by this dreaded snake.

< Surprised by rain in the middle of the forest, Boca plaits palm leaves into a protective roof for Awaenca and her baby. With a touching gesture, she wipes the raindrops off his back.

The fascination of these primitive people is inescapable. Their way of life is rooted far back in the history of mankind, and only little has changed over the centuries. Far removed from the questionable progress of our technological civilization, forgotten by time, they live in jungle isolation in perfect harmony with their environment.

The young Auca's games prepare them for their future duties as hunters. For the moment they catch only butterflies, lizards and small birds, but soon they will be allowed to accompany their fathers or uncles on minor hunting expeditions and to shoot at monkeys with curare-poisoned darts for the first time.

>
Apa and Cincawae have had a successful hunt. They step out of the cool forest into the clearing heavily laden with spider and howler monkeys.

Pages 121–128
Growing children are given a great deal of
freedom so that they can develop their own
personalities. They are very rarely punished.
They become familiar with their environment through games. They amuse themselves
with animals captured by the hunters, with a
little woolly monkey or a bat that they have
found in the frame of the hut. Innocent of
cruelty, they play with a lizard, tying a string
round it and torturing it to death, or with a
furry bumblebee, fastening a delicate chambira fibre around its leg and whirring it
round their heads like a small live airplane.
They swim, fish, play in the clearing, wrestle
or build a marvelous slide on the river bank
in the wet clay.

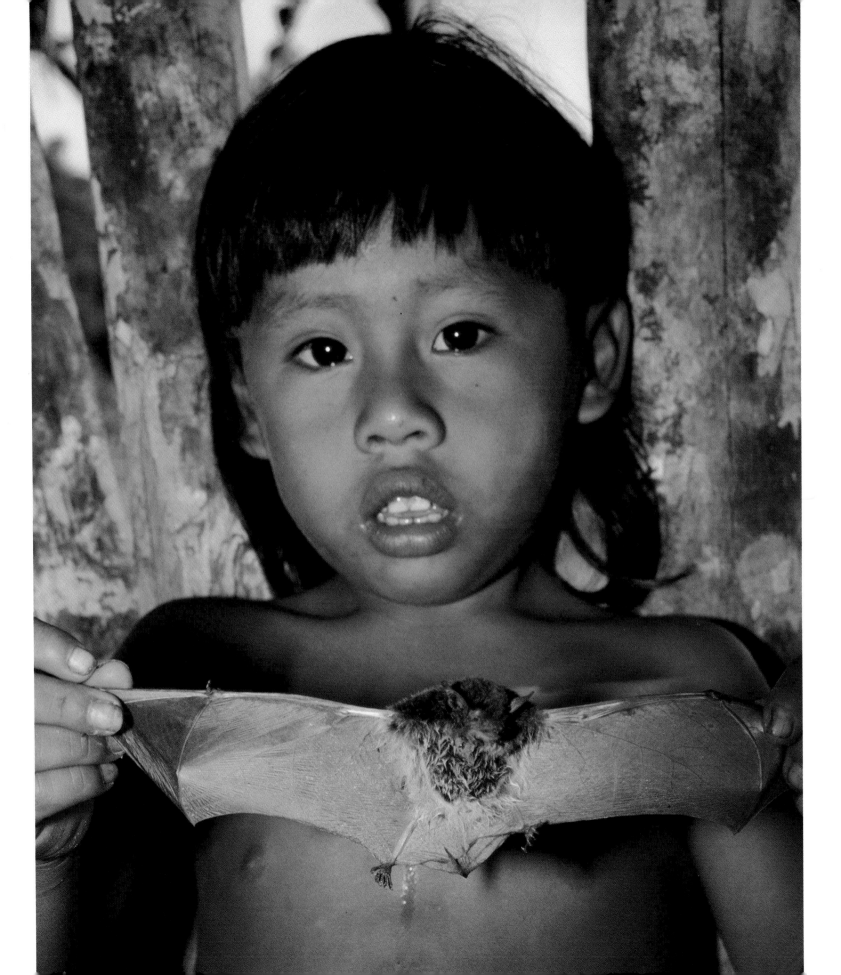

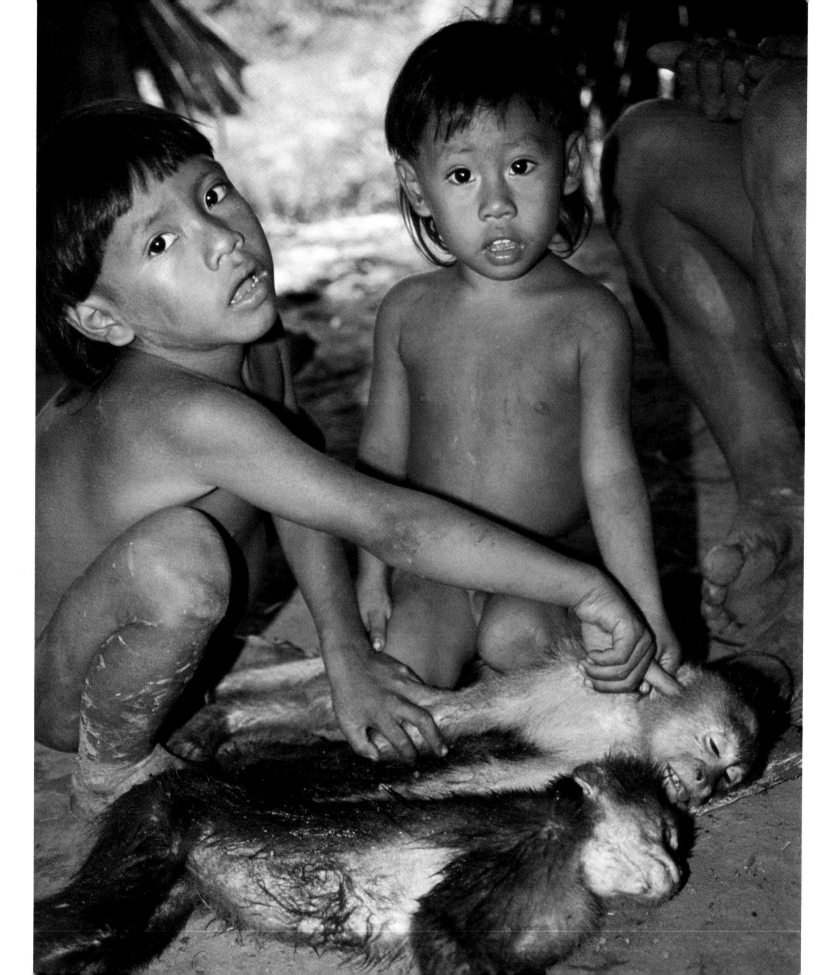

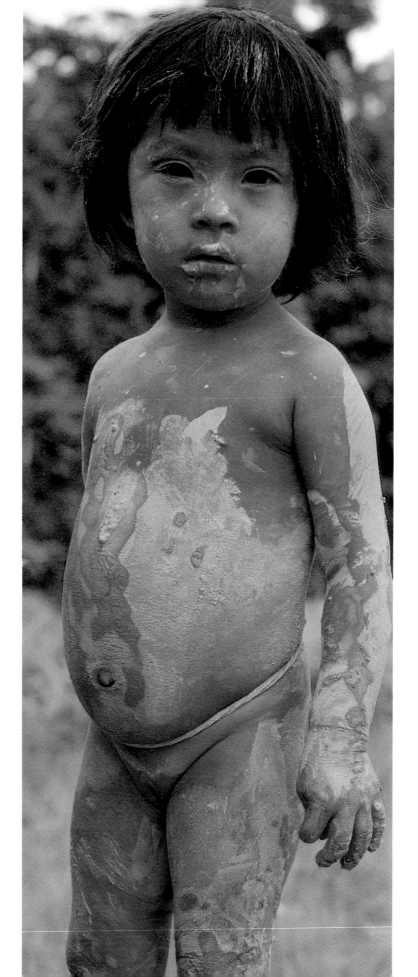

Weevil maggots: an unusual delicacy!

into our coffee-cups and wait until we are ready to go and visit their new huts.

Last year's communal hut is close to collapse: the leaves are rotting and the trunks have been gnawed by termites. Menga has built a new one for his family directly next-door. Though she is hardly older than forty-five, Omamo, a grandmother of eight, looks small and weary; her skin is wrinkled, her breasts hang down slack and flat. She is squatting by the fire, busy with a hind leg of a peccary, which is hanging in the smoke. "Waaquiwimi, Omamo?" – "Waaquiwimopa, Pero!" She is already feeling better, and the children are rid of their fevers and lively again.

Fifty meters further up, the trail leads directly through Caruae's new hut. It, too, is solid and clean, with a high ridge beam and palm-leaf-covered roof sloping down to the floor. It smells of smoke and rancid bacon. And as usual, there is the normal confusion of hammocks, spears, blowguns, quivers, nets, baskets, Chambira fibres hung up to dry and large clusters of green bananas. Cacadi has had her first child, a girl; she is about seven months old and has been named Omamo after her grandmother. The last time we visited them, Ñawanae had also been pregnant, and we ask about her baby. "We killed it – it was a girl," answers Caruae.

"Eh, éh," confirms Ñawanae dispassionately. "We had to kill it because it was another girl." If two girls are born consecutively, the next daughter is killed at birth, usually by strangling her with a liana noose. A newborn infant is also often killed if the child that preceded it is not yet weaned, although the information we received on the subject was not quite clear. In any case, both of these criteria applied to Ñawanae's baby[3]. The explanation is simple: it was another girl, and they already have three in the family. Awancamo is their only son; girls are a burden; who is going to marry them? Caruae needs sons. Sons become hunters and bring the monkeys home! Caruae's solution is cruel but effective. He knows only the laws of nature: they encompass the powers of good and evil; and when Caruae strangled his new-born infant to death, he did what was expected of him and what he himself considered right.

We balance our way across long, thick, fallen treetrunks to the last hut, which is even higher up and deeper in the forest. It is not constructed in the usual way, the whole front of the hut towards the clearing having been left open from the bottom to the very top. This is where Apa, Boca and their families live. Camemo's daughter, Bogewai, the first child to have been born at the Cononaco, has been renamed after my wife in the

[3] As soon as we arrived a year later, Giicabae brought us her new baby, which was only a few weeks old. She pointed proudly to his penis: a son! After two daughters, a son! Boca has only had daughters by his second wife, Awaenca, too, so a further female child would have been killed at birth, and Giicabae would have bowed to his judgment. It should perhaps be mentioned that population control by selective infanticide is an old custom in various primitive Indian tribes.

meantime, even if the unpronounceable Wally has become Wangi in the process[4].

In the afternoon Sam distributes the rice to the four families and gives them advice on how to sow the peanuts and corn. We have brought along some gifts: little, metal toy airplanes with tiny wheels and propellors that turn delight the children, though some of them ultimately end up among the men! We have necklaces of tree-fruits and glass beads for the women. The necklaces are not worn every day, most of the time they are carefully stored in a basket in the hut. The men get new machetes. The South American machete has been their most important all-purpose tool for a long time – even the smallest fragments are used – and belong irrevocably to their modest material culture now. Stone tools and Chonta-wood knives have been forgotten because for years the Auca have managed to procure machetes and steel axes either by violence or otherwise. It is a pity that ugly, dented aluminum pots have lately found their way into the Auca hut as well and are slowly but surely replacing their clay pots.

We have brought a dozen colour photos of our last visit, but no one seems very interested in them. The fact that they look at a picture upside-down does not seem to bother them at all. Soon the photos are lying unnoticed and crumpled on the floor and become toys for the children. But the pictures of strange people and animals are greatly admired. Their questions about pictures of elephants, giraffes and Massai dancers are endless. A picture of New York is so far beyond their conceptual grasp that it is hardly paid attention to, and a NASA close-up of the moon with a corresponding explanation is accepted as completely natural. Menga is particularly impressed by a pair of Bengal tigers from the Basle Zoo. For a long time afterwards the photo is fixed to the crossbeam over his hammock with little wooden sticks, and he never seems to tire of studying it in great detail.

Every morning our macaw wakes us up with his noisy replies to the screeching of his wild counterparts as they fly in pairs from their sleeping trees to their feeding places in the first rays of the sun. We do not have to wait long for Wadi, who feeds it a handful of boiled rice or manioc, its customary breakfast. With Wadi come the first children. At first they stand quietly, whispering reverently around our hammocks, then they start getting impatient and noisier, pulling at our hammocks and robbing us of our last precious moments of sleep until we finally have to get up and heat water for our first, indispensable cup of coffee.

4 Wangi died of a high fever 8 months later. Apa and Camemo took us to her grave in an old, deserted hut at the edge of the manioc garden. A small clay pot of chicha with a palm leaf over it marked the spot of tamped earth. Camemo's eyes filled with tears: "This is where we buried Wangi. Her head lies where the sun rises. That is where she came from and that is where she returned. Wangi is in heaven, but her soul comes back and drinks chicha." – If the Auca find the chicha pot empty on the second day after the burial, they believe the soul of the deceased has given them a sign that someone else in the family is going to die in the near future.

The spider monkey, with its exceptionally long extremities, is the master acrobat of the jungle. This trapeze artist propels itself rapidly through the treetops, swinging from branch to branch, always grabbing one branch with its prehensile tail and swinging upside-down to the next. It often bombards intruders with branches and shows its anger by barking or giving piercing shrieks.

Every day brings us new impressions and experiences: for example, when we accompany them on their search for wild honey. It is amazing to see how confidently Apa can find his way back to the spot in the dense jungle where, coming back from hunting a few days earlier, he had noticed the entrance to a beehive high up in a tree. Now the Wipita tree trembles under the loud, echoing strokes of his axe until it slowly begins to tilt where it has been notched and then thunders through the undergrowth to the ground. Once again the shavings fly, and soon the beehive, imbedded in luminous pink wood, has been uncovered and the small, black, stinger-less bees swarm angrily out of the gaping hole. Dark, egg-sized bags filled with liquid honey cluster around the combs. The Auca slurp the sweet jungle nectar with relish and noisily lick drops of honey from their fingers. The rest of the comb is carried home in a leaf basket neatly trussed with bark fibers.

Or when they break open the bark of a palm rotting on the ground to look for yellowish-white, almost 1-cm-thick weevil maggots, which are considered a special delicacy either raw or baked in hot ashes. It is only very hesitantly that I manage to overcome my original revulsion and contemptuously take a little of the titbit I am offered: it tastes like lightly smoked bacon.

Or when Menga demonstrates how to make a fire in the age-old manner of his ancestors. He crouches in front of a small dry board into which several holes have been worn and which rests on two pieces of wood. Into one of the holes he inserts the tip of a fire drill consisting of a half-meter long, slender shaft. He twirls the shaft rapidly between his palms until the heat of the friction ignites the wood. Now, as he carefully blows at the embers, small blue tongues of flame appear and leap over to the nearby cotton tinder and dried-up stems, until a few moments later crackling red flames appear out of the smoke.

Or when, in the heat of the afternoon, the clouds gather into the blackness of a thunderstorm, the wind chases a wall of water over the forest, and soon nothing seems to exist but the angry pelting of rain. When flashes of lightning illuminate the jungle and thunder resounds deafeningly through the forest. When the water rises in the riverbed and beats against the bank, and in its brute force the current tears bushes and whole trees out of the ground, turbulently pulling them under and letting them reappear, spinning and shooting through the frothing waves and disappear again behind the lashing rain!

Or when the sun sinks into the jungle in the evening and the clouds on

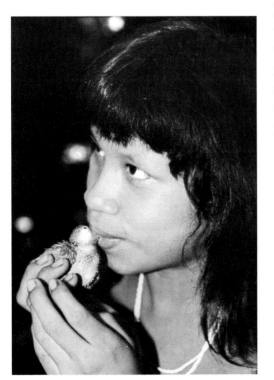

Young parrots are fed manioc gruel directly from their keepers' mouths.

the horizon catch fire. When fireflies flit through the bushes, sending sparks flashing against the roofs of the huts. When the reddish-yellow crescent moon rises behind the silhouettes of treetops and the night is black and cool, the sky clear and starry. When we lie in our hammocks hearing the Auca in the distance singing in their huts; and when still later, all that can be heard is the mournful, melodious call of the tinamou.

Again and again the return of a hunter is a fascinating experience. His long oval blowgun shouldered, his bamboo quiver and shiny black calabash sphere dangling from a chambira cord around his neck, he steps out of the cool forest. If he has caught nothing or his take is meager, he walks up the path quietly and inconspicuously and disappears into his hut. But if he has been successful and crosses the hot clearing with two or three monkeys slung over his shoulder, he stops at our hut, laughing. There is pride in his eyes as he goes enthusiastically into every detail of the hunt. Often it is fat, curly-haired woolly monkeys that he drops on the ground, or long-limbed, hairy black, spider monkeys, and once even a living monkey baby only a few days old, clinging to its dead mother's fur in panic; or one or two heavy, sturdy, reddish-brown howler monkeys with swollen larynxes; or a few of the smaller, light-furred capuchin monkeys. The Auca do not scorn small squirrel monkeys or night monkeys either, even hunting marmosets, which when adult are no larger than a human fist. Apart from peccaries, which are particularly desirable, they also hunt squirrels, coatis and armadillos. Among the birds they like to hunt are various kinds of turkeys, guans, curassows, toucans, macaws and many others, whose names we do not know.

One afternoon Menga has a special surprise for us. There is a big, brown, long-haired bundle hanging from the mouthpiece of his blowgun: to our joy and amazement it turns out to be a two-toed sloth, the strangest tree-dweller of the tropical rain forest. As it lies in the grass, its sickle-clawed feet trussed up with lianas, we take a closer look at it. It pulls faces, bares its teeth and stares at us with red eyes full of hostility. Suddenly, in spite of its bonds, it rears up, hisses and, with a quick, unexpected jerk, tries to bite my hand. Then, exhausted by the unaccustomed strain, it sinks back into the grass again. The Auca are not particularly fond of sloth meat, so after I have photographed it from every angle, we set it free again. Liberated from its bonds, it drags itself to the trunk of a cecropia tree, its movements grotesque as if in slow-motion, its stomach sagging, and ever so slowly claws itself further and further up until it disappears upside-down into the treetop.

The small path leading from the end of the runway up to the huts can be clearly distinguished. Menga has built a new hut next to the communal one, which, attacked by termites, is close to collapse. A bit further up, the path runs right through Caruae's hut. Apa's and Boca's families live even deeper and higher up in the jungle. At the lower edge of the picture, the 'guest house' that Boca and Cincawae built for Sam and that we, too, use on our later visits.

Then there is the time that Menga brings a baby howler monkey scarcely a week old, which had survived the fall from a tall tree still clutching its dead mother's fur, back from the hunt. Now, separated from its mother, the little monkey shudders with every sigh it heaves until it discovers the surrogate fur of Giicabae's hair. When it has calmed down and its heart-rending ú-huh-ú-huh has died away, Giicabae carefully places the trembling creature to her breast. After a few unsuccessful attempts, it finds a teat, greedily begins sucking it and then starts observing the new environment with black, liquid eyes. Or there is Boca, who brings a young owl from the forest. It has the beautiful, long-lashed eyes of a prima donna, and its feathers are still downy. It, too, joins the Auca menagerie. In the evening, still afraid and hesitant, it grabs the tail of a lizard it is offered, but obviously does not yet know quite what to do with it.

No hut lacks captive wild animals. They belong to the household. Apart from monkeys, there are mainly birds like macaws, parrots, parakeets, hawks and owls. As they are kept tied to short horizontal poles with chambira cords, their lives cannot be considered enviable. But children take tame woolly monkeys and spider monkeys outdoors as playmates and young women carry them around on their heads and nurse them like their own infants. A few magnificent macaws fly around free, too. When they are called, they fly to the hut, land on someone's shoulder and then gravely perform elaborate acrobatics on his outstretched arm to get to a piece of manioc they are offered. My question as to whether this zoo might, so to speak, serve as a living meat supply in bad times is answered emphatically in the negative; and when a little woolly monkey is found dead at the end of its lead a few days later, it does not find its way into the pot but is carried into the forest and buried there by Wadi.

Unfortunately they have no harpy eagle, whose wonderful, soft, black and grey feathers the Auca value very highly. They like to keep these eagles captive on high, covered platforms as mascots. Menga's harpy did not survive the move to the Cononaco, and up to now no one has been able to bag another one alive.

As long as there is enough monkey meat, the Auca seldom think of going fishing; they leave hook-and-line fishing to growing boys. Another traditional way of fishing – with poison made from crushed barbasco roots, which paralyzes the fish and allows them to be caught with one's bare hands as they float dazed, stomach up, down the river – is possible only in calm, shallow water; the rapid, deep Cononaco is, of course not suited to this method. We have brought along steel hooks and fishing lines from Puyo, and now Boca and Caruae want to try them out. Awaenca and Cacadi, both with their infants in a baby-sling, and the young fishermen Bainca and Nontowae accompany us as we go down the narrow trail in the burning heat and then enter the pleasantly cool forest behind the last hut. In the semi-darkness one could imagine oneself in the silence of a medieval church. The air is heavy with humidity and the peculiar though not unpleasant smell of earth and rot. Everything growing in those many overlapping layers is reaching for light. The thick roof of interlaced leaves and palm fronds permits only a small amount of sunlight to penetrate to the damp, moldering ground. Grass grows between light green ferns and young plants shooting out of the ground. Philodendrons sprout out of cushions of moss and twine round smooth-barked, white-speckled trunks. Bright fronds project from young palms, and between the huge leaves of a heliconia, drops of water glisten on a large spider-web. Lianas as thick as a human arm hang from the trees, twining thick arteries around the high treetrunks and winding and weaving like wires in the branches. Huge, rotten trunks lie across the trail, the wood shot through with holes made by termites. An emerald-green lizard scurries across the bizarre prop root of a palm, and a large, indescribably beautiful iridescent-blue morpho butterfly flutters through the twilight. The upper stories of the forest are formed by large, more sparsely growing, broad-topped trees and, even higher, the sunlit, leafy domes of giant trees standing in imposing isolation, their broad branches covered with air plants that make them into veritable hanging bromeliad and orchid gardens.

Silently the Auca lead us through the labyrinth of trees, their flat, broad feet and strong, spread toes gripping the slippery trail. They glide nimbly over mossy treetrunks, cross streams, wade through small swamps and leave us far behind – clumsy, slipping, stumbling, sweating and cursing. When we catch up with them beyond a slight elevation, they are just procuring fish-bait; several dead birds are already lying on the ground. Boca puts his index finger to his lips as an admonition to be quiet. Bainca blows clear, mournful birdcalls on a leaf clasped firmly in cupped hands, and calls a bird closer. A few steps behind him, halfhidden in the tangle of the bush, Caruae pushes a white-spotted dart into the mouthpiece of his blowgun, aims it almost vertically and puffs up his cheeks to shoot. Seconds later a small, feathery bundle reels out of the branches and remains twitching and cheeping on the ground, the dart through its throat.

Caruae aims his blowgun almost vertically, distends his cheeks to blow and seconds later a bird comes reeling through the branches to the ground, where it lies twitching, a whitedotted dart through its throat.

They pass the time fishing at an old river bend that has become a calm lake. Although fish brings welcome variety to the Auca menu, it has only modest significance as a source of protein.

Our destination is a broad, old river bend that has become a calm lake, its glassy surface bordered by banks thick with vegetation. A cayman, only its eyes and snout above water, is startled; giving its tail a violent buffet, it dives out of view. Thousands of butterflies flutter up from the loamy, wet bank in a yellow and white, dancing cloud. An hour later there are a dozen fish lying on the bank, among them a circular stingray with black spots and three piranhas, which have been rendered harmless by a quick, spine-snapping bite in the neck. Then a sudden cloudburst forces us to set off for home again. In a very few minutes, Boca has considerately plaited a palm-leaf canopy to protect Awaenca and the baby from the rain, while Caruae silently and unconcernedly makes his way home through the downpour with his wife and child. Halfway home, Boca points to hand-sized paw-prints clearly visible in the sodden ground: "Meñe, meñe ...waene, waene, ii!" They are jaguar prints! Boca is worried and drives us and his wife through the forest until we get to the clearing and can catch our breaths again.

Shortly before dark we hear the eerie cough of a prowling jaguar, and the next day Menga unexpectedly comes across it in the forest. At the end of his hunt, Menga had wanted to return to collect a few howler monkeys he had killed, covered with palm leaves and left under a tree. Suddenly he found himself face to face with the jaguar, which had been attracted by the smell of the dead monkeys. It had already devoured one and was about to start on the second. Without his spear, Menga would never have dared to take on a jaguar. But now, with the jaguar snarling and preparing to spring, angry because its meal had been interrupted, Menga did not hesitate long and rammed the spear into its side. Soon the badly injured jaguar gave up the fight and retreated into the bush, the spear still firmly imbedded in the wound. Menga tried to follow it, but found only his bloody weapon a few hundred meters further on.

Writing and drawing are unknown to the Auca, and we are eager to see what will happen when we give them crayons and paper. They go at their task with great dedication, and we are astonished to see that, independent of one another, their own impulses lead all of them to the same form of expression. They cover one sheet after the other with closely spaced squiggles and horizontal zig-zags or wavy lines. We are perplexed until we realize that they are using the crayons the only way they know how to: to write with! They have frequently watched us writing in our diaries, and so their astonishingly similar scribbling is nothing but an attempt to imitate our writing. It is only much later that

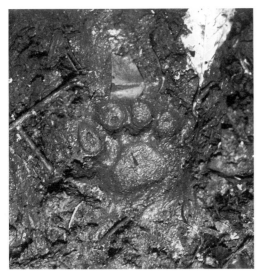

A jaguar's fresh pawprints can be clearly made out in the damp earth of the forest.

Bainca one day spontaneously breaks away from 'script' and begins depicting 'caterpillars, beetles, leaves and trees' in hieroglyph-like symbols. But only after we have demonstrated other representational possibilities do they succeed in producing spontaneous, unspoilt little works of art in which they record their visual impressions of their environment intuitively and imaginatively.

We spend hot afternoons sitting in the shade of a hut, asking the Auca many questions. Our way of seeing their life is inevitably influenced by our own standards and logic and much that we observe must remain superficial. It is not easy to penetrate the intuitive, seemingly illogical world of the Indians. They are part of the natural world in which they live. In their cosmos, the borders between the natural and the unnatural, between reality and myth, are blurred. And the language barrier makes everything even more complicated. Our rudimentary knowledge is not sufficient to express more subtle ideas, so we are dependent on Sam to translate. But he, too, is an Indian and often has trouble formulating the thoughts of another world in precise English. I find it particularly frustrating when, after an Auca has talked on and on, Sam's translation is limited to just a few brief words. They seem to enjoy our questions and answer all of them willingly though not always immediately to the point.

"How did the world come into existence, Menga?"

"Waeñongi created the world a long, long, long time ago. Waeñongi brought the trees, water, all the animals and he brought the Auca."

"Who is Waeñongi?"

"I don't know."

"How does he look?"

"I don't know. No one knows."

"Like a fish," says Camemo.

"No," objects Boca, "like an Auca. He has big holes in his ears, just like an Auca."

"Mba, mba," – no, no, – insists Menga, "we don't know. At first there was no forest. One could touch the sky with one's hands. Fire came from the sky. All Auca who had not planted manioc died. And a great deal of water came. They took lianas and tied themselves to calabash trees which did not break, and the water could not carry them away, and they lived."

"But we do not know anything about Waeñongi. He is not in the sun. The sun rises and rises all the way up and comes down and goes up again on the other side, like the moon."

The Auca have gathered in front of Caruae's old hut for a celebration. Holding up bundles of macaw tail-feathers, the men sway forwards and backwards untiringly and stamp to the rhythm of the freshly cut, single-pitched bamboo flutes. During breaks in the dancing a calabash full of chicha is passed from one mouth to the next.

Scattered feathers glisten in front of the hut where bagged birds have been plucked. Particularly beautiful specimens, like delicate toucan breast-feathers, are carefully stored away. The hunter will be using them for a headband later.

>
Mima is working on a new hammock. These sleeping nets, which the women knot out of chambira cords, demonstrate great technical skill.

With the help of his wife Cacadi and his eldest son Awancamo, Caruae needs three days to build his new hut. The solid framework of young treetrunks is lashed together with jungle vines. Later he will weave tight layers of broad, dark-green leaves into the transverse ribs of long palm fronds to complete the waterproof roof that slopes from the 4-meter-high ridge beam to the ground.

The tame scarlet macaw belongs to the Auca
household. Now and then it interrupts
its flights to walk gravely round the hut in
search of something edible.

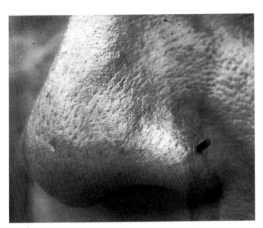
"Pass-holes for the trip to heaven."

"Our land is here in the forest. This is our land. From here to the other hut, from there to the other hut, across many rivers to Tiwaeno. Where the sun sets there is a wide river, and that is where the Cuwudi live. All the strangers."

"And beyond the river?"

"I don't know. There the sky meets the ground. There is only earth. It is nothing. Nothing more. There are no trees. Only earth."

"Where do the Auca come from?"

"I don't know. My grandfather knew. He said they had come down from the hills many many years before. Far far up, from where the river comes. There were many Auca, but now there are only a few of us left."

"When I die, I will go up, high up, until I meet all the people who have died. There is a huge thick worm, as thick as a tree, on the narrow trail that leads to heaven. The worm sees the earplugs and knows that these are Auca coming. He doesn't let anyone else through. It is better still if one has holes in one's nose." Menga's nostrils have a small perforation on either side. With thumb and index fingers, he pulls the short, sharp splinters of chonta-wood that are inserted in the openings to keep them from growing together out of his nose and proudly shows us his 'pass-holes for his trip to heaven'.

"The dead climb over the back of the big worm and can enter heaven. The ones the worm doesn't let through have to go back again. They rot and become termites."

"One lives well in heaven. There is plenty of monkey meat and as much manioc as one can eat."

Neither Menga's nor Titae's group have a shaman at the moment, and questions about the Iroi, the witch-doctor, bring only vague, hesitant replies:

"Wi m'ponimopa." – I can't remember.

"Nampawae is an iroi. He is old and lives at the Yasuní. If I were ill, I would not go to him. We are our own group!"

"When he drank ayahuasca[5], strange voices came out of his stomach. He knew where the peccaries were and told us: go here and go there. And we found the peccaries. But we were not allowed to spear their leader, for it was his own jaguar."

"He is none of our concern."

But the question about forest demons causes lively comment on all sides:

"Wenae, the devil of the forest, comes in the night. He sucks out your blood until you die."

5 Banisteria caapi, a hallucinogen.

"The owl knows when he comes. Sometimes he comes disguised as a small bird with a blowgun and sometimes as a black jaguar."

"Cuwudi suck each other like the devil."

Hearty laughter. Boca purses his mouth and leans over to Awaenca, who draws away in mock indignation. They have made their point: Cuwudi are strange creatures!

"We are afraid of the Cuwudi when they come with their noisy blowguns. The old people say: 'Be careful, strangers are bad, they must be killed!'"

"When I was a child, my mother told me: 'Be quiet or the Cuwudi will come and eat you up!'"

"We are also afraid of the big snake. It is an evil devil. Whoever kills it must drink hot water and stay in his hut for three days without eating meat, otherwise little anacondas will grow in his stomach and he will die."

"We fear the Tageiri[6]. They come in the night and kill us with their spears. But we kill them, too."

"Why?"

"That's how it has always been."

"My father was speared to death," says Apa. Apa's father Kai was suspected of having caused the death of a young Auca who broke his neck falling from a tree because of an evil spell.

"My father was also killed with a spear," say Camemo, "and my mother died of a bushmaster bite."

"When was the last spear murder?"

Now everyone talks: "When the chonta fruit was ripe, before we lived here. Copae and Apurae, who lived with us, killed a Tageiri. He was an old man. Twice the moon became big before the Tageiri came for revenge. They came with their hammocks and said they were coming for a visit. But we knew that they wanted to kill Copae and Apurae, but they were not with us. They waited and waited, but Copae and Apurae did not come, and then they lost patience and speared Nimonga and fled into the forest."

Cincawae throws an invisible spear and with a grimace of pain points to his stomach and puts the other hand to his back saying, "And the point came out here, and the next day Nimonga was dead."

Enough talk of killing. "Boca, how many wives may a man have?"

Hearty laughter among the women. Boca, somewhat embarrassed, says, "Three, but two are enough. One has to shoot down many monkeys for

Head ornaments made of harpy-eagle, heron and macaw feathers.

6 A militant Auca group in the region of the Tivacuno and Tiputini rivers.

the women and children. Two are enough, but Apa and Menga have only one wife each. I have two because they are sisters."

But now Boca is the first to get up and leave the hut. "Idawa, gobopa!" – I've had enough! Soon the whole group is frolicking in the cool Cononaco like boisterous children.

It is hard not to be fascinated by these primitive yet wonderful people. Their way of life is rooted far back in the history of man, and little has changed through the centuries. Far removed from our technological civilization, hardly touched by its questionable progress, forgotten by time, they live in total harmony with their environment. In their timeless present, there is no ambition, no anxiety about the future, which does not lie much further ahead than tomorrow's hunt. Their thinking and behaviour are spontaneous, natural, uncomplicated and unembarrassed.

Even though blood relationships and style of life tie them to the group, they live as free, independent individuals within the community. Perhaps precisely this apparent contradiction between the goals and constraints of the community, which necessarily help determine individual behaviour, and the opportunity for the individual's self-realization provides an explanation of the success of the simplest imaginable, egalitarian, prehistoric form of society.

We have not encountered jaded, brutish savages, we have discovered sensitive people with a sense of humour and individuality, with good and bad traits as they can be found in people everywhere. But the Auca do not interfere in each other's affairs. Whether Uruka is fat and lazy is no one's business but her own; whether Apa wants to go hunting today or tomorrow or laze in his hammock for hours is his business alone; no one minds if Boca prefers to walk around in an old pair of shorts; if Naenquiwi cannot resist the temptation of the missionaries and takes his family to the Reservation in Tiwaeno, and even if he then decides to return to the Cononaco, no one expects him to justify himself – they simply welcome him back. Everyone acts the way he is and is accepted as such by the group with neither praise nor blame.

Private spheres of personal life hardly exist. No one is alone. The happiness and unhappiness of a lifetime take place in front of the same circle of ever-present spectators. Everyone knows everything in a way that we would find possible only in a very small village. And people have a lot of time for one another: they laugh and talk, naively carefree; they pick lice out of each other's hair and insects from each other's bodies. Free from anxiety about the future, free from material worries, they have an ability we envy them for: they can enjoy the present with genuine, animal contentment.

They do not recognize any institutional authority apart from the laws of nature that regulate their lives and determine their fate. Only their dependence on the rhythm of nature subjects them to constraints that allow of no alternatives.

No one gives them orders. They have no chief, and their language has no word for the function either. A primus inter pares might be possible: a Titae or a Menga, who, owing to his age, experience or great skill as a hunter, stands out from the rest of the group and may be asked for advice. There are no courts and no judges. Punishment for a wrong, whether real or imagined, is the business of the one who feels he has been wronged. Often there are only two choices – forget the incident or kill the alleged offender. Brawling and swearing are unknown. One begins to understand why they do not carry grudges in connection with minor, everyday occurrences, why certain things that would make us angry or even livid with rage are simply received with disarming laughter here.

They know nothing of envy, jealousy or theft, and the Auca language has no words for these concepts either. How could it, in a society that knows only the unavoidable differences of age and sex. The forest belongs to everyone, and the opportunity to use it is equally open to everyone. What little the Auca possesses he has taken from the forest: wood for spears and blowguns, clay for pots, chambira for hammocks, poison for darts and feathers for headbands. Their technology requires neither specialists nor complicated processes or tools: every family can produce all the things it needs independently and find the raw materials to do it in the immediate surroundings without any great difficulty. The Auca can do everything, and that is why his daily life is anything but monotonous. But the fact that his stock of material goods is limited to what is really necessary and useful leaves him a great deal of leisure time, something that might make superficial observers reproach him with laziness.

Our technology may awaken their curiosity, but seldom their admiration. With their unerring sense for what can be of immediate use, they show great interest in machetes, steel axes, candles, matches, combs or the hammocks we have brought along.

Their thoughts and senses are chiefly channeled towards the vital aspects of life: hunting, food, safety, sexuality. Abstract ideas are foreign to

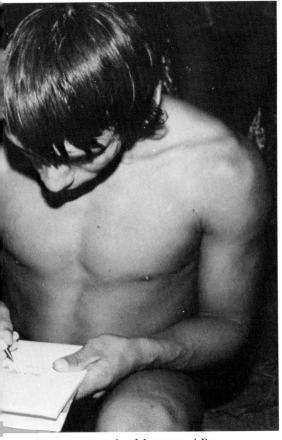

As soon as we give Menga and Boca paper and colored pencils, they settle down to their new task. The result are spontaneous, naive works of art in which they express their environment intuitively and imaginatively.

them. To know, one must see, hear, touch, smell, taste. Thus their religious world is uncomplicated, too. They believe in the power of the invisible, in the magic of the forest, in the legends of their ancestors and in the power of an unfathomable creator-god. Traditions and customs have been passed down through innumerable generations and they believe in them without questioning, without brooding, for ...that's how it has always been.

Even if integration in the community is to some extent emphasized in bringing up children, the most important aim is the future independence of the adult individual, especially, of course, of the man. Child-raising is casual and unrepressive. Growing children learn by their own experiences and by observing the adults and their environment every day. They grow up in a carefree, easy-going atmosphere and are subjected to as little discipline as possible, which allows their own personalities to develop freely. During its early years, however, a baby is constantly looked after by its mother or an elder sister and is never left alone. It is taken everywhere in a baby-sling and sleeps in its mother's hammock at night. The child feels safe in the gentle care and constant proximity of its mother. Several times a day it is deloused and washed; it plays with little pet monkeys or is tugged from its hammock by its sisters and often hugged so hard it almost suffocates.

When a child is weaned, often only in the third year of its life, the reins are loosened and the child begins to explore the world on its own. Toys in the actual sense of the word are unknown. Children play with leaves or pieces of wood. They pass the time with animals: bats discovered in the framework of the hut, turtles from the river or lizards that are caught, tied up and innocently tortured to death, or furry bees around whose legs they tie chambira fibres and have great fun whirring round their heads. Children swim, fish, romp in the clearing, try to stand on their heads, improvise wrestling matches or build slides on the loamy river bank.

A daughter becomes aware of her future role early in life. Even before she is sexually mature, she gradually begins carrying out the tasks of daily life. She fetches water from the stream, brings firewood, plucks birds, peels manioc, looks after younger brothers and sisters and learns to weave baskets and do everything else expected of her later as a woman. The boys fish, learn to whittle darts, practice using the blowgun and are pleased when they start to bag butterflies and lizards as their aim improves. They accompany their fathers on lesser hunting expeditions and are soon hunting their first birds on their own to use as fish-bait or to feed the owl or hawk, whose care they have taken over.

We never see children quarrel and rarely hear them crying. Omamo seems unconcerned as her two-year-old son Yata sits next to her playing with a sharp, pointed knife. But her attitude is conscious, never losing sight of the aims of Auca up-bringing: if he cuts his finger, he will learn about the danger of a knife. Only rarely does a father hit a child with a bunch of nettles or a liana because it has been disobeying its mother all day. But when Apa beats seven-year-old Tewae with the penis of a peccary-boar, it is to help the boy grow up to become a good, courageous hunter. Have I now described the 'bon sauvage' with the virtues of the noble son of the wilderness so highly praised by the Romantics? That was not my intention. The romantic idealization of the Indian and a way of life that may awaken feelings of nostalgia in us but we can never return to ourselves is as far from reality as contemptuous portrayals of the Auca as horrible, unfeeling spear-murderers.

The last day always comes, whether we like it or not. In the early afternoon there are cries of "Ebo, ebo!". Soon we hear the hum of engines and the glittering dot in the blue sky grows larger and larger: the Cessna! Capitán Rosendo Flor has kept precisely to his timetable.

We have promised to fly Menga, Boca and Cincawae over the area where the Yasuní group lives. They have relatives there – Menga even has a brother – whom they have not seen for years. On foot a visit would require many long, arduous days of walking, which they do not want to risk since they are no longer certain of where the group is. Flor agrees, and so Sam and I get the three Auca, who are trembling with excitement, into the plane and we fly north over the Cononaco. Twenty minutes later we find an airstrip cleared by missionaries, Cawaro Airstrip, alone and deserted, like a light brown scratch in the green of the forest. Not a hut to be seen, not a soul. We search to the west, we search to the east; finally, not far north of the central course of Rio Yasuní, Boca discovers a plume of smoke and we head for it. Soon we see an opening in the jungle and in the middle of it, among a confusion of fallen treetrunks, a large, elongated hut. On our second, lower, and even lower third flight over, Menga and his friends recognize the old witch-doctor Nampawae and Menga's brother among the half dozen naked figures standing in front of the hut waving for us to land. What we would do for a helicopter now! We find three more huts scattered in the area, and we see larger and smaller groups of Auca standing and gesticu-

Visitors in our hut.

lating up at us with excited faces. We estimate that there must be about 25 Auca in the group.

A good hour later we are back at the Cononaco. Our three heroes have been rendered nearly speechless by their adventure, but they bask in the admiration of the others. In the meantime, Wally, Apa and Caruae have gotten our baggage ready for take-off. It is hard for us to say good-bye. We do a lot of back-patting and promise to return. As the Cessna lifts off, the Auca stand in the shade of the hut waving good-bye to us: two dozen naked 'savages' who have become people with names, faces and feelings. They grow smaller and smaller until they finally vanish in the jungle.

Cincawae's drawing could be entitled 'Auca on the Cononaco'. The stylized figures have not been sketched indiscriminately, for days later the artist still knows exactly whom each one represents. At the top right, a trumpeter bird with wings and claws; next to it, at the edge, five monkeys easily recognizable by their prehensile tails. At the left there are spears with feather ornaments.

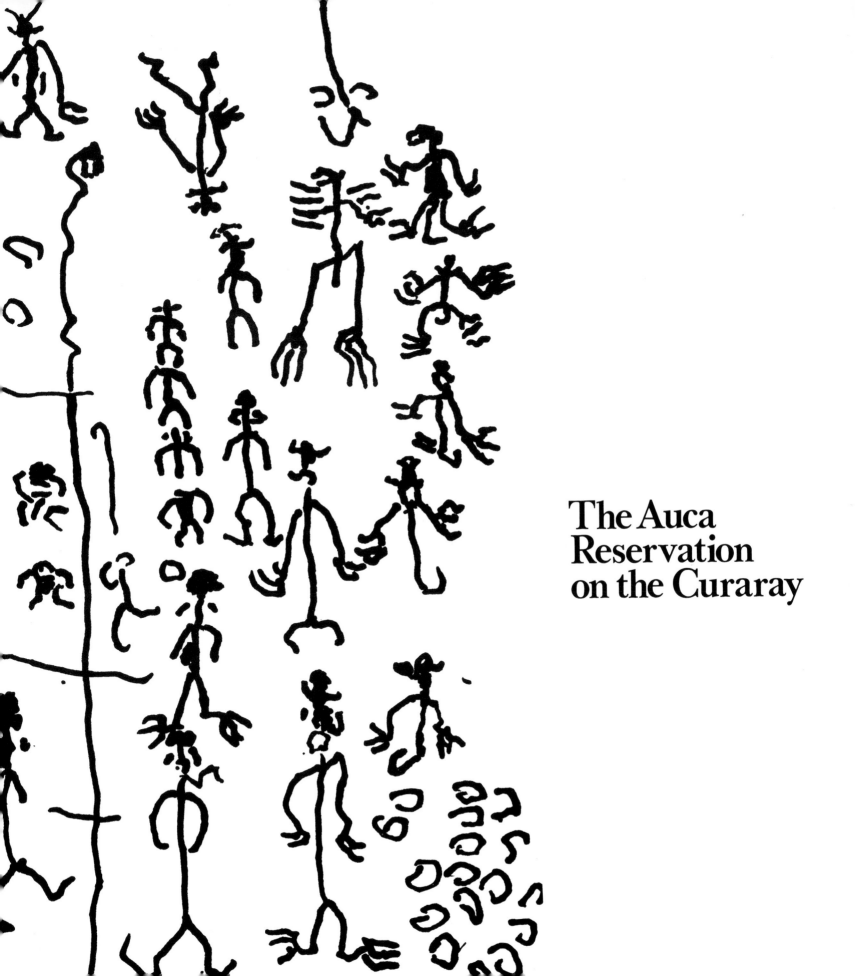

The Auca
Reservation
on the Curaray

The approximately 1200 sq. km reservation declared 'Zona de Protectorado Auca' by the Ecuadorian government in 1968 – with the eager approval of the Linguists – lies northeast of Puyo. Bounded by the Nushiño River in the north and the Challua River in the south, it is divided into two about equal parts by the Rio Curaray. This is where 500 missionarized Auca involved in the questionable process of acculturation live, crowded into a fraction of their original territory. They have been sucked irrevocably into a world they do not understand. Though they had not been seeking to join the march of progress of our civilization, they are nonetheless paying a high price for it: abandoning traditions thousands of years old and thus renouncing their cultural heritage.

The outpost of the Linguists from the American Wycliffe Bible Translators missionary group responsible for the Auca reservation is in Tiwaeno. This worldwide Protestant group is well-known as the Summer Institute of Linguistics. It has a well-trained staff of over 3000, making it by far the largest and most energetic U.S. mission. It has set itself the task of missionarizing small, forgotten and isolated tribes in remote corners of the world. The starting point of their work is language, which is the key to their attempts at establishing contact with these so-called primitive peoples. Their goal is evangelizing infidels through the New Testament liberally translated into their native tongues.

They believe they have heard God's call and let nothing get in the way of their task: Go ye therefore, and teach all nations.

They see as a more profane justification of their activity the necessary preparation of the Indians for their inevitable encounter with civilization. They want to protect them from its most harmful influences and the consequent social uprooting, and are supported in this by those who are convinced that a tribe is lucky if it comes into contact with missionaries before being confronted with oil prospectors, lumbermen, road construction teams and other intruders. The Linguists in Ecuador do not doubt that the march of technological progress and the drive to open up undeveloped regions of the jungle together with the growing demand for oil will inevitably have to lead the Auca into a crisis of survival which they would not be in a position to weather on their own. The missionaries consider it their Christian duty to spare the Indians the trauma of future cultural shock or at least to alleviate it significantly. They have always held the Auca to be unhappy, primitive savages with barbaric customs – above all infanticide and polygamy –, who must spend their miserable lives in constant fear of their tribesmen's spears.

What was not accomplished by the Jesuits in the 17th, the rubber tappers around the turn of the 19th and the anthropologists, oil prospectors, hacendados, adventurers and soldiers of fortune of the 20th century was achieved by a pair of women possessed by religious zeal: on October 8, 1958, the legendary Linguist missionary Rachel Saint and her co-worker Betty Elliot established the first peaceful contacts with an Auca group.

In February 1955, Rachel Saint, with the help of Dayuma – the Auca girl who, frightened by her tribe's spear feuds, had fled to the Rio Napo – began deciphering the Auca language at Don Carlos Sevilla's hacienda 'Ila'. Using the index-finger method and her first rudimentary phonetic notes, Miss Saint was able to establish a provisional grammar and a simple dictionary. She felt she had been called to the untouched Auca tribe and prayed she might be successful in "transforming the primitive, fear-ridden heathens into believing Christians through the power of the Gospels." She soon realized that the young Dayuma could be the key to establishing contact with the Auca and that Dayuma's influence could be used to convert the rest of the tribe in a kind of 'snowball effect'. Not even the massacre of the five young North American missionaries in 1956 (among them her own brother Nate Saint and Betty's husband Jim Elliot!), who died by Auca spears near a sandy bay on the Rio Curaray during their first attempt to make contact, could divert her from her plan.

In July of the following year – the world's attention had in the meantime been drawn to the unfaltering missionary – she was invited to Hollywood with Dayuma. Thirty million people watched Ralph Edwards' popular television program 'Rachel Saint, This Is Your Life!'. Months later, evangelist crusader Billy Graham extended an invitation to Rachel Saint and Dayuma, giving them the opportunity to talk about "the heathens lost to the powers of darkness deep in the Ecuadorian jungle".

The first breakthrough came in September 1958. Dayuma had managed to establish contact with her former family group. She brought back from her visit not only endless reports of more spear murders, but also the news that her group was willing to receive Rachel Saint and Betty Elliot. Only a few weeks later the women, accompanied by Dayuma and Betty's four-year-old daughter Valerie, set off on their arduous expedition through the jungle by way of Arajuno. On the third day they reached the 56-member Auca group on the Rio Tiwaeno whom Dayuma had fled from 12 years earlier. For Miss Saint the moment for which

she had been preparing for so long had finally come. She wrote to a friend: "The Lord has chosen this tiny spot to highlight for the world many tribes being reached by missionaries, unseen and unsung, too busy with the job at hand to write home about it." And now, as Ethel Wallis later described: "Dayuma, who now taught her people God's carving, oriented them also in their relations to a larger world. She was drawing aside the forest curtain and expanding their limited horizons."

Step by step the missionaries, supported by the over-zealous Dayuma, were successful in overcoming the Indians' original mistrust. The message of the Gospels was first met with lack of comprehension, mockery and rejection, then with doubt and insecurity. Gifts achieved better results. Skilfully, methodically and with unbelievable patience, the women pursued their goals until the Auca's natural resistance slackened and finally broke down. Their newly learned feeling of shame led them to start wearing clothes, and their earplugs, which had now become symbols of heathen barbarism, disappeared. Confused, rendered insecure, their traditional order disturbed, the new order not understood, the Auca at Tiwaeno had allowed themselves to be caught unawares and to become the core of the new evangelistic conquista in Ecuador. A palm-thatched roof over a simple wooden platform became their first church, and soon a school was standing next to it. By the time Miss Saint was able to send the Auca translation of the Gospel of Mark to the printers and a year of hard work had seen an airstrip cleared in the jungle, the seven palm-thatched huts had become a Linguist outpost and the first wedge had been driven firmly and irrevocably into the Auca forest.

In spite of the missionaries' persistent efforts, the other Auca groups vigorously resisted further attempts at contact, however. Then, in the mid-60's, the Linguists found powerful allies: the oil companies. After the fiasco experienced by Shell, who had found no oil and retired from Ecuador in 1951, prospecting firms were returning to the jungle; and with the 'Lago Agrio No. 1' drill hole, the Texaco-Gulf consortium established beyond doubt the existence of significant oil reserves in eastern Ecuador. The Auca seemed to be sitting on oil! The problems Shell had had with them were only too well known. So it was natural that the Linguists' missionarizing endeavours were not only approved of but actively supported. Those bothersome savages had to be gotten out of the way as fast as possible, and the least one could do was to place airplanes and fuel at the Linguists' disposal. Everybody except the Auca, whom nobody bothered to ask, was happy: the linguist who wanted to

Dayuma's 'Ochococha' settlement.

save the Auca from hell, the oil companies that wanted their profits and a government long embarrassed by the savage tribe, which would finally be able to have them all under control on the reservation.

Of the new methods employed in trying to make contact with the Auca, one was of decisive importance – the systematic use of the 'basket transmitter': a radio transmitter was hidden in the false bottom of an Indian basket and an antenna inconspicuously worked into the plaiting. Then the basket was filled with gifts and dropped to the clearing where the Auca lived with a nylon parachute. While the plane circled above the dropping point, the Linguists remained within the transmitter's range, making direct contact with the Auca by means of headphones, microphones and loudspeaker. It is not difficult to imagine how enormous an impression the mystery of the baskets – in conjunction with the booming voice from the metal bird overhead that called them by name, answered questions, gave instructions and promised further gifts – must have made on the Auca. So it should not come as a surprise that, after repeated dogged attempts, the Linguists finally succeeded in 1968 in attracting a new, large group to Tiwaeno, thus doubling the number of Auca living there from one day to the next.

But the problems soon doubled, too: flu epidemics spread through the Indian settlement in recurrent waves, and the terrible consequences of a food crisis could only be avoided by flying in CARE packages. The hunters had to go further and further into the jungle to find game, and finally there were hardly any monkeys and birds left. New chicken coops were looted, the manioc plantations robbed and the Tiwaeno proselytes set upon on all sides by the distraught, unruly newcomers. The new Christian ethic began shaking in its foundations, and the missionaries could not keep the worst excesses of the heathenism they so abhorred from spreading nightmarishly through the village. Despite all the difficulties, a new group was brought to Tiwaeno in August 1969. Two weeks later disaster struck: a polio epidemic broke out, leaving 16 Auca dead and as many crippled in its wake! Bamboo crutches and wheelchairs became an integral part of life in the jungle clearing. This traumatic experience led to the total collapse of a world the Auca were no longer in a position to understand. Baiwa, speaking for one of the larger groups, called Tiwaeno 'a place of death' and left the reservation with half of his people.

In November 1969, the contact flights that had been halted temporarily during the polio epidemic were started again! The Linguists' unwavering faith in their mission kept them from having any doubts about their methods. They did not learn from their mistakes. "The most important thing is placing the Holy Scriptures into the Auca's hands," stated a letter from the head of the Mexican branch of the Wycliffe Bible Translators to Rachel Saint. The high density of population in Tiwaeno for Indian conditions was unquestionably the greatest mistake the Linguists made. But it is hard not to suspect that all this was done intentionally. By tying a large number of Auca to Tiwaeno and the immediate vicinity, the missionaries achieved effective supervision, preventing relapses into their former way of life and thus avoiding the danger that the Indians could slip from their grasp again.

Contact with civilization became unavoidable.

Above all there were more and more confrontations with acculturated Quechua Indians living in the border areas of the reservation in the Arajuno region and further north on the Rio Napo. The example of their material culture awakened new desires: steel axes, rifles, rubber boots, salt, sewing machines, canoes, radios ... and the growing wish to possess objects thus far unknown generated new problems. For centuries the Auca had been able to take advantage of their environment in a way that never endangered the ecological balance. Species-conserving hunting in small groups had prevented the forest from being overtaxed. Now steel axes, rifles and dynamite provided new and dangerous influences which – especially in connection with an unnatural concentration of population in a comparatively small area – threatened to be disastrous to the Auca. The basic problems that arose on the reservation may be summarized as follows:

– Concentration of the population in relatively large, permanent settlements caused the system of social and political equality, which had proven itself in small family groups, to begin deteriorating.

– The surrounding forest was soon hunted bare. There was a protein deficiency. The principle of self-sufficiency began to falter. For the first time, nature had left the Auca in the lurch!

– The imposition of a doctrinaire religion led to the collapse of traditional cultural values.

– The growing demand for consumer goods, which could not be obtained from the natural environment, resulted in the development of social distinctions and thus envy among those without property.

– The integration of new groups caused tension; old hostilities flared up, creating new danger of spear feuds and personal vendettas.

Without Dayuma's help, the first Auca group could not have been missionarized in 1958. But in Tiwaeno they did not find the happiness they had been promised by the Linguist missionaries. Their new life on the reservation brought them only disease and hunger. Dayuma, bitter and disillusioned, led some of her people to a new location on the Rio Curaray.

– The outbreak of diseases against which the Auca had not yet developed natural immunity had disastrous effects.

– Dependence on the Linguist staff increased (food, salt, medicines, vaccines, snake serum, munitions, clothing, tools, schooling, religious worship, allotment of places to live, etc.), while the Auca's own will to be independent and free diminished.

It took the Linguists years to get some sort of a grip on the situation again. Unruffled despite their setbacks in Tiwaeno, they organized an impressive multi-media show in 1971. They presented the Auca who had taken part in the killing of the five North American missionaries as converted, God-fearing, new Christians to large American audiences in cities from Dallas to Chicago and Rachel Saint solicited contributions and support for her mission in Ecuador with unflagging zeal.

Disillusioned and discouraged by what had happened, Dayuma and other leading Auca began to take groups of their people away from Tiwaeno and resettle them in other parts of the reservation, thus weakening the Linguists' control. Most of the 8 to 10 groups living on the reservation today are known by the names of their leaders; four of them are women: Dayuma, Wipe, Olga and Wiñami, who have, as a consequence of the situation, instituted a matriarchal system. The total number of Auca living on the reservation has grown to a little more than 500, while the number of free Auca has dwindled to hardly more than 100.

To judge living conditions on the reservation we had to have a chance to observe them first hand, so we were happy to accept an invitation from Dayuma, who was, of course, particularly looking forward to seeing her son, Sam, again. On our return from the Cononaco, we stayed at Joe Brenner's Turingia in Puyo again and made preparations for our visit to Dayuma's Auca settlement on the Rio Curaray, in the middle of the reservation. The Quechua call it 'Ochococha', and it is located only a few minutes by canoe from where the five missionaries were slain by Auca spears in 1956. After two attempts rendered abortive by the weather, a Cessna finally got us to Tiwaeno on a hot, humid, November afternoon. At a bend in the narrow, crystal-clear Rio Tiwaeno, a dozen palm-thatched huts line the grassy, hardly 200-meter-long landing strip; in front of it, a clearing has been cut into the jungle. The noise of the engine drives a small herd of zebus apart and white herons fly out of the glistening field. As we taxi to a stop, a large crowd of Auca is standing there, ready to greet us. We are immediately conscious of the contrast their outward appearance and shy, almost suspicious, manner make to that of the Auca we know from the Cononaco. These Auca make a strangely depressing impression, and we see in their eyes the resignation and sadness of people who have been transformed from Indians to Indios. Their clothing ranges from gym shorts and T-shirts to torn shirts and unwashed, ragged, calico skirts. Pego, who had led us through the jungle in search of an anaconda on the Cononaco only a year before, greets us with an embarrassed, wistful smile. He has folded a headband out of an old newspaper, his ears hang empty without their balsa plugs, his dirty, yellow T-shirt advertises Japanese bicycles and his feet are in cut-off rubber boots two sizes too large for him.

Rachel Saint, who is 66 today, has retired from the reservation. Her old house, built on stilts with a wooden platform, split bamboo walls and palm-leaf roof, stands deserted. Here we hang our hammocks among the spider-webs and decaying witnesses of the past: from a chamberpot through chairs without seats and old calendars to a dusty first-aid kit with dried-up ampulles in it. We see nothing of the Linguists; and their new house, built across from it in a similar style, is empty.

Early the next morning we start off into the jungle in the steaming morning mist. Sam's stepfather, Komi, a rifle slung over his shoulder, a broad machete in his hand, leads us and a line of eight Auca carrying our baggage and other things intended for Dayuma, among them a blackboard for the new school, down a narrow trail through the luxuriant undergrowth. At the Rio Yuwiwaeno, a tributary of the Curaray, a long dugout canoe is waiting to take us and our things downriver to Dayuma.

Komi stands at the bow, rhythmically punting the boat down the river with a long pole. We glide softly through the calm water, over glittering, sunny surfaces, through the shadows of huge trees that form dark tunnels over the water with their long, projecting, bromelia- and orchid-covered branches. Turquoise kingfishers sparkle among the roots of dead treetrunks sticking out of the water, and every now and then a startled wild duck flies out of the tangle of vegetation on the bank and escapes downriver with flapping wings. At the Curaray, the water flows wide and muddy yellow over rapids and sandbanks. Crowded on the narrow, hard benches, our limbs painfully stiff, we are mercilessly exposed to the burning rays of the sun, the bloodthirsty flies and the annoying black wasps. The dream-like romance of the jungle is over, and we are left with the torments of a long, uncomfortable journey by canoe.

A newly discovered sense of shame makes original, natural nakedness seem offensive. But the ragged, unwashed clothes of this Auca woman and her daughter on the Tiwaeno Reservation make one thing depressingly clear: the new 'citizens' of Ecuador belong to the country's lowest social classes.

> The first day of school in the jungle! Faces washed, wearing their Sunday best, the Auca children from Ochococha sit at their unaccustomed desks in the new school and listen to their Quechua teacher with a mixture of mistrust and fascination in their eyes.

Auca girl on the Tiwaeno Reservation.

House-pets are looked after on the Curaray, too. Even puppies vie with infants for mothers' breasts.

Class distinctions in the Auca community on the Curaray show in the various styles of life. The simple hut of a family that has only just moved there contrasts conspicuously with Dayuma's roomy house, with its corrugated iron roof, Singer sewing-machine and short-wave radio.

Cawaeno was flown from the Yasumi group to the Tiwaeno Reservation by the Linguists barely two years ago. Today, although he feels safe from Tageiri spears here, he regrets his decision. For the photo he has exchanged his tattered blue-jeans for a hip-cord and taken out his old headband with beautiful harpy-eagle and macaw tail-feathers.

>

Gikita lives on the Curaray. At the age of about 60, he is an old man according to Auca standards. He has about a dozen spear murders on his conscience. When the five young, American, Linguist missionaries were massacred, he was the leader of the attacking group and threw the first fatal spear.

This old Zaparo woman has found refuge with an Auca family half an hour upriver from Ochococha by canoe. She is assumed to be the last survivor of an Indian people that still numbered 100,000 in the 16th century. Starting with the arrival of the Spanish Conquistadores, contact with the western world has brought the Indians only misfortune and destruction.

A large crowd of Auca welcomes us in Tiwaeno. We are immediately aware of how shy, almost mistrustful, they are and how their outward appearance contrasts to that of the free-living Auca we know from the Cononaco.

After seemingly endless hours, we finally reach our destination in the late afternoon. Tired and stiff, but happy to have the tortures of river travel behind us, we wade to the bank, where we are received by a noisy, colorful crowd of Auca. Dayuma stands unmistakable in their midst, laughing and welcoming us. She is just as we had imagined her: in her late forties, small, stocky, in a colorful cotton-print dress, sturdy legs in heavy rubber boots, straight black hair parted in the middle and falling over her shoulders, and the resolute look of someone who is used to being respected. A path running alongside a manioc garden takes us to a large clearing. In the middle of it cluster about a dozen huts. Some are on stilts, others are constructed in the Auca manner with high ridge beam and roof sloping down to the ground. Most have palm-thatched roofs, but a few have the ugly, corrugated, sheet iron roofs that are unfortunately so common in the tropics. Dayuma leads us to the guest house, a simple platform open on all sides with palm-leaf roof. It is only a few meters away from a clear stream that winds its way round the settlement. There are ducks, geese, turkeys, woolly monkeys, macaws and dogs quacking, screaming, squawking and barking everywhere. With the excited chattering and giggling of the Auca crowding around our hut and the increasing cool of the evening – the sun now just a red disc above the trees – we get a second wind, and feel relieved to have left the depressing atmosphere of Tiwaeno behind us.

The Auca make a healthy impression. They are unconstrained, natural and – with their own Auca sense of humour – laugh a lot. But somehow they seem to have lost their close bonds with nature, and not much is left of the candour and simple, unspoiled dignity of the free forest Indian. Transistor radios blare the latest hits from Quito, supplanting the Auca's own ancient refrains. Rifles are beginning to replace blowguns. The latter, together with quivers and darts, are still carelessly produced in large number, but are now regularly sold to souvenir dealers in Arajuno, from there finding their way to the curiosity shops of Puyo and Quito. Monkeys, birds, armadillos and peccaries have become rarer, and the men seem to have to make do with one hunting expedition a week.

In the evening, an Auca limps into the clearing supported by his friends. He has been bitten in the foot by a bushmaster. Dayuma injects her last snake serum by the light of my flashlight. In the middle of the night we are awakened by yapping dogs chasing an ocelot that has ventured to approach the chickens in the moonlight. An hour later the dogs, barking angrily again, lay a heavily bleeding opossum in front of the hut.

The next morning heralds an important day in the life of the Ochococha settlement: the new school hut, with its plastic Ecuadorian flag flying over the roof, is to be inaugurated. The two Quechua teachers arrived a few days ago with notebooks, schoolbooks and pencils. The younger teacher is even sporting a tie in honour of the occasion! Now young and old come crowding curiously round the entrance of the school-house. We have counted 97 of them. The schoolchildren, faces washed, wearing their Sunday best, look for their seats: 13 girls and 17 boys between the ages of about 12 and 15. They learn their first words of Spanish during their first lesson. The teacher has written them neatly on the blackboard; now they slowly repeat after him in chorus, again and again, louder and louder: "Mi patria se llama Ecuador!" – "My homeland is called Ecuador!"

The house Dayuma's family lives in is conspicuous because of its size and more solid construction. Apart from a modest supply of medicines and a Singer treadle sewing-machine, it also has a short-wave transmitter, helping Dayuma keep in touch with the outside world, especially with the Linguists in Tiwaeno. Closer to the forest, several groups of families live scattered in seeming isolation in simpler, Auca-style huts. They are far shyer and more taciturn, and they wear less or sometimes hardly any clothing. Social distinctions have arisen. The Ochococha hierarchy ranges from Dayuma's leader caste at the top down to the total have-nots. The new form of society has created affluence and poverty, satisfaction and discontent. Differences come out in housing and clothes, for even the scale of footwear ranges from barefoot through torn sneakers, plastic sandals and patent-leather shoes to rubber and leather boots. While most of them still sleep in hammocks, some can already afford a mattress. The rifle has become a status symbol, the blowgun has been demoted to the old-fashioned weapon of the simple man. The proud possessor of a transistor radio pales with envy when his neighbor turns up with an impressive radio that has short-wave bands.

The food supply seems to be more or less safe, for the nearby gardens provides enough manioc and bananas. The loss of protein resulting from the continual decline of game is compensated for by river fish, which the Auca get from the Curaray and small tributaries every day. Dayuma is planning to introduce pig-breeding in the future, and Sam is already thinking of the possibility of flying in milk-cows later.

The group is busy clearing a runway in the jungle under Dayuma's supervision. The men use their steel axes on the trees while the women clear the ground of undergrowth with machetes. Dayuma has yielded to the Linguists' pressure: in a few months the isolated settlement will have an important, new bridge to the outside world.

On long evenings we sit in our hammocks in the flickering candlelight, listening to Dayuma's captivating stories. She tells us about her childhood in the Auca forest; about the forest demon who sucked the blood and life out of her grandfather's forehead; about the old witch-doctor who had power over the jaguar and the anaconda; but also about never-ending spear feuds, which her father, brother, uncle and countless other relatives fell victim to; about fatally injured men buried alive with a son or daughter, their screams becoming fainter and fainter until they were silenced completely by the weight of the earth above them; about her own escape from the jungle; about her life on the hazienda 'Ila' and her encounter with Rachel Saint; and much about the sad events at Tiwaeno.

Her greatest worries are the many illnesses that occur and her lack of medical supplies. She complains bitterly that the Linguists had abruptly stopped providing medicine and snake serum free of charge and that she now has to pay for everything, even aspirin. "I have so many orphans here, but I don't even get free medicine for these innocent creatures! We have to pay for clothing, too, even if it is old and worn out. It is unjust, because I know that these old clothes are collected in the U.S. Of course, the settlement makes some money by selling blowguns and other souvenirs, but it's not enough. Many people, particularly the older ones, pay me with fruit and monkeys, and I just don't know how to pay my bills." She does not like talking about other problems she has with the Linguists and cleverly manages to evade our questions again and again.

After a week has gone by, Komi and a few other men take us back to Tiwaeno. We want to avoid as much of the long, strenuous journey up the river as possible, so after two hours in the canoe, we get out and follow the Auca who are walking ahead, carrying our baggage on tumplines and occasionally slashing lianas and thorny creepers out of the way with their machetes. The trail is slippery and can hardly be made out in the confusion of the jungle. Our first hour in the oppressive humidity leads up a hill, and climbing on muddy ground saps our strength. After a 6-hour hike, we finally reach the Tiwaeno clearing weary and dried out. In the meantime the Linguists have returned. We say hello to Catherine Peeke, the linguistic researcher and Bible translator, and to Rosi Jung, a graduate midwife of German descent, who works as a practical nurse. They welcome us with cool, refreshing lemonade. The third Linguist, Patricia Kelly, who supervises the school, is down with malaria and has retired to her hut.

They have bad news: their radio reports that the Pastaza runway is closed for repairs for a few days and that our pilot, whom we were expecting tomorrow, disappeared to Quito over the weekend. Convinced that Captain Flor would not leave us in the lurch this time either, we had left our food supplies with Dayuma and now have to share our last cans of tuna, boxes of cookies and half a dozen tea-bags and then live on the smoked fish and manioc the Auca provide until one of the Linguists' Helio Courier finally takes us to Pastaza four days later.

In Tiwaeno, Rosi Jung gave us the Linguists' version of the problems described by Dayuma. She confirmed the fact that medicine, clothing and other necessities had been given to the Auca on the reservation free of charge until 1976. But she said it was wrong and ultimately irresponsible to let the Auca believe in manna falling from heaven through God's grace. It was part of the process of acculturation to make them understand the value of money – in fact, some of them were already quite good at handling it. They were now paid for producing souvenirs; if they could buy radios, rifles and munition with this money, it was only right for them to get used to paying for medicine and clothing. That this policy would meet with opposition came as no surprise to the missionaries, and they realized that it was not easy for people like Dayuma, who were responsible for a comparatively large group, to collect the necessary money. Medicine was sold at a 30% reduction, and the expensive snake serums from Brazil were to a large proportion paid for by the Linguists.

A later conversation with Don Johnson, the dynamic director of the SIL in Ecuador, allowed us to conclude that a few significant changes in their thus far rigid views were in the offing. They finally seemed to have come to the conclusion that a high degree of dependence on their field personnel was leading the Auca into an increasingly dangerous situation of not feeling responsible for their actions. Now the Auca were to be given greater freedom so that they would have a chance to solve their problems themselves! The Linguists now also agreed that dividing the Auca population among several smaller settlements within the boundaries of the reservation was a better solution. Personal contact with their field personnel was restricted to a very few visits to the Auca settlements each year, and education by their staff was reduced by about half. The Auca were now being encouraged to organize their own schools and

On the reservation manioc also plays an important part in the production of chicha, a sweet, very nourishing, milk-like drink. While the chicha cook is crushing the root tubers into pulp, she frequently takes a mouthful of manioc, chews it carefully and spits it back into the pot. By this process the enzymes in her saliva cause the chicha to ferment slightly.

were allowed to put in for aid from the government program for Indian education, which, as we had seen, had already been done by the Ochococha group. The Linguists do remain unyielding on one point, however: they continue to work towards their goal of missionarizing the Auca and will find no peace until the last free Auca is on the reservation!

Anthropologist Jim Yost maintains that since 1977 the Linguists have realized that positive future development will be possible only if the community of Auca living on the reservation and their own leaders manage to find creative solutions to the problems they are facing by gaining inner strength. But the amount of initiative the Auca themselves can bring up depends on the growth of their knowledge, their resources and the interaction of reciprocal relationships[1]. In the sphere of the modern Catholic mission, this view has already prevailed for some time, Catholic missionaries tending far more towards preserving existing traditions and culture and not aiming primarily at the acculturation and conversion of primitive peoples to Catholicism.

According to Yost, one of the greatest problems for the Auca is that they have accepted the Quechua living on the borders of the reservation as their model of civilization and now mainly want to have consumer goods like the Quechua's. The Auca hardly realize that in reaching their goals they would be giving up even more of their identity. Not only would integration into national life unavoidably put them in the lowest Ecuadorian social class; being considered barbarians by the other Indians, too, they would be condemned to the lowest rank on the Indian scale and reduced to subsisting in humiliation, frustration and privation. In this connection, Yost asks himself whether the committed anthropologist should stand by and watch or even help them to reach a goal they have set themselves although he knows that its realization would ultimately have devastating effects, or whether he should try to dissuade them from their plan and try to steer them towards other objectives.

The question of whether missionary activity spares primitive peoples a traumatic confrontation with an intolerant civilization, merely delays it or even hastens it will probably remain controversial for a long time to come. One thing is certain: the methods used by Protestant missionaries in Ecuador were badly chosen: and the Auca that were so unscrupulously herded onto the Tiwaeno reservation have not been spared the shock of clashing cultures. The motives of the Linguists' much-criticized collaboration with Texaco-Gulf also remain questionable, for they have undoubtedly promoted their own interests through it.

1 Cuaderno Etnolingüístico, No. 6, SIL, Quito 1979.

It remains a fact that the huge forests afford the last free Auca enough space to survive. In the last ten years, only the Tageiri Auca group has stood up aggressively for its own independence and thus come into serious conflict with oil interests.

Ethnocide, the destruction of the cultural values of a people, whether consciously and systematically or accidentally and unintentionally, does not just start with forcible expulsion from traditional tribal lands or with the construction of roads and runways that bring civilization dangerously close. It also begins when simple, primitive peoples are confronted with a system of beliefs they cannot grasp; when ancient traditions and ways of living are condemned as barbaric customs and a doctrinaire form of Christianity wants to become the sole guideline for thought and action. It starts when a newly discovered sense of shame makes people cover their nakedness with tattered shirts, when the forest Indian trades his simple tools for the machete and steel axe and the rifle replaces the blowgun. But it also starts when – out of pride or shame – governments become aware of their exotic minorities and want to integrate them into the national culture, whatever that means. The alienation of their values begins when their language is devaluated to a

On long evenings we sit in our hammocks, listening to Dayma's captivating stories in the flickering candlelight.

dialect, when the national language is learned and when the national flag is flown over a palm-thatched roof. Even assimilation that was originally well-meant leads forest Indians inexorably and irrevocably to the abandonment of their freedom, of a life in intimate contact with nature and in its worst form to the robbery of their land, to the exploitation of their labour and to the prostitution of their women. Then, when their backs have been broken, they sink rootless and unstable into decadent social and racial misery, and only a very few manage to make a successful transition to modern life.

Naenquiwi has populated his forest with monkeys, coatis and squirrels. He first explains the tree-like figures in the lower half of the picture as Auca, later he insists they are 'tall trees', and finally he cannot exactly remember anymore: "Wi m'ponimopa." Naenquiwi was, by the way, born with six fingers on each hand and six toes on each foot.

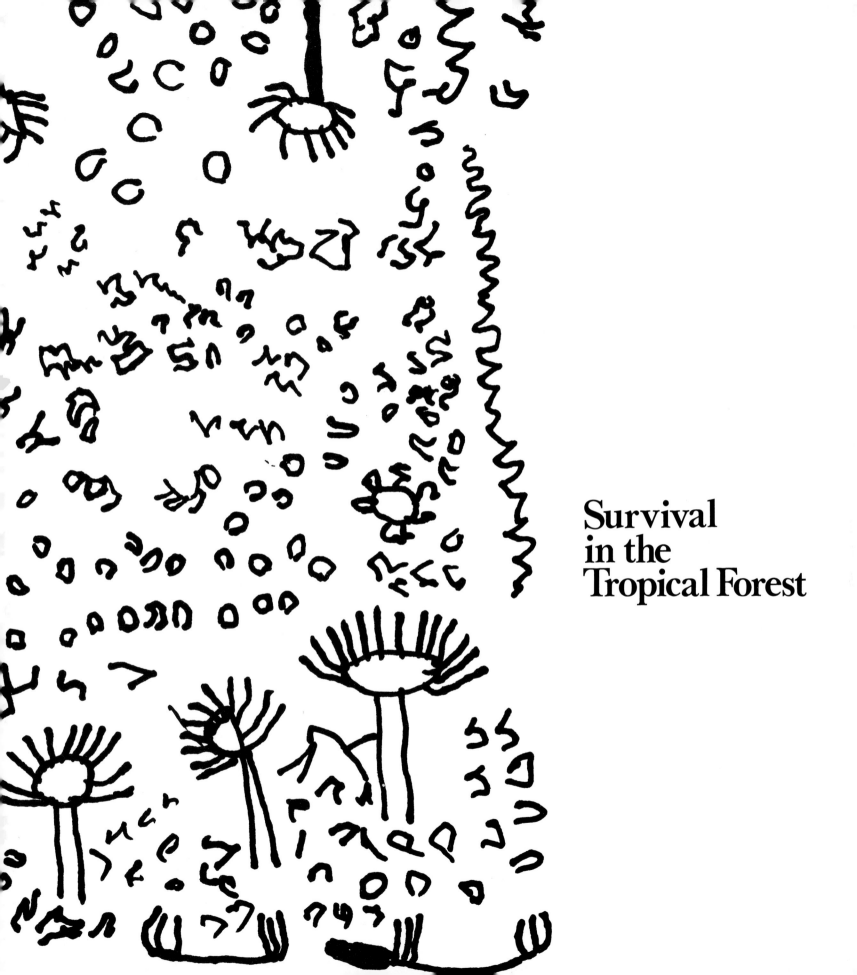

Survival
in the
Tropical Forest

Do the last free Auca still have a chance to survive?

In Brazil the systematic extermination of Indian populations by the 'civilizados' of neocolonialism with machine-guns, dynamite, poisoned food and clothing systematically contaminated with smallpox was the routine method of dealing with the indigenous population. Though the FUNAI (Fundação Nacional do Indio), South America's largest-scale Indian foundation has been established, the solution to the Indian question remains highly problematic. The long-term goal of Brazil's Indian policy is the assimilation of its Indian peoples into national economic life. Ultimately there are to be no Indians left, only Brazilians! The FUNAI cannot successfully work against the national goal, so one of their most important tasks is to see to it that the Indians do not become an obstacle to the development of Amazonia. To the makers of Brazil's economic policies, it would be unthinkable for an insignificant Indian minority to block the approach roads to the region, thus jeopardizing their ambitious colonialization projects.

Nonetheless, an attempt to break out of the vicious circle has come from Brazil. It is thanks to the exemplary initiative of the Villas Bôas brothers that in 1961 the Brazilian government created the 22,000 sq. km 'Parque Nacional do Xingú' in northern Mato Grosso, thus saving the Indians living around the Xingú River from complete annihilation. 16 tribes with 6 different languages and a total population of about 1800 live in Xingú Park today. Although it has already been criticized as a 'human zoo' and 'anthropological hallucination', its creation remains a bold alternative to many other, usually inadequate, attempts to solve the problem of the forest Indian. In contrast to FUNAI's goal of assimilation, the Villas Bôas want to safeguard the surviving, though severely decimated, tribal Indians by securing their land rights within the framework of a reservation to which outsiders are largely denied access. In this protected environment – missionaries, too, are barred from entering the reservation – not only the physical survival of the Indians is to be guaranteed; their way of life and ancient customs are to be preserved as well as possible, too.

Under the conditions prevailing in Ecuador today (especially if one considers the discouraging state of its forest Indians, such as the Quechua, Shuara, Cofán, Secoya, Záparo and reservation Auca), the Villas Bôas' alternative seems to be one of the few remaining effective solutions for the survival of the free Auca. It should serve as a guide to everyone concerned with the Auca question, above all the appropriate Ecuadorian government authorities. It would not require the considerable financial resources needed, for example, to protect the endangered animal world of the Galapagos Islands. It would 'only' need the understanding and good will that would enable Ecuador's last primitive Indian people to be spared from total and final annihilation.

The solution seems almost too simple: safeguarding the Auca groups living in their original state by guaranteeing their land rights within the framework of a reservation from which outsiders are largely barred. That means:

– The creation of a protective zone on the Cononaco which grants the Auca genuine collective property on their traditional land and thus expressly guarantees them the sole legal right to use its natural resources. The area and borders would have to be established with due regard to the Indian ecosystem and possible population growth. It should, within limits, correspond approximately to the geographical situation of their traditional territory. The incorporation of an uninhabited buffer zone to avoid future conflicts, and which could at the same time serve as a biological preserve to protect the flora and fauna, would be ideal.

Roughly it would be a matter of three to four thousand square kilometers west of the 76th meridian, extending north from a strip of land south of the Cononaco to the headwaters of the Rio Yasuni.

– The unrestricted right to their cultural and ethnic autonomy without government or missionary interference.

The reservation should not become an open-air museum. In order to avoid unnecessary contact with civilization, it should also be closed to tourism.

– An important condition would be the independence of the Cononaco Reservation from the existing 'Zona de Protectorado Auca' around Tiwaeno. A separate solution suitable to the circumstances would have to be sought for the future of the Auca living there. The question of appropriate supervision of the reservation will necessarily arise. An independent, egalitarian community closed off to the outside world can hardly, if at all, take a stand on the outside world. Even if the reservation had to be placed under the patronage of the Ecuadorian government, the responsibility for respecting the rights of the Auca should be placed in the hands of a small, legally constituted group of guardians who have thorough knowledge of the Auca's way of life. Sam Padilla, who has close ties to their culture, speaks their language and is one of the few to have remained in regular contact with them, would certainly seem predestined for the job. The guardian group would also include representatives of the appropriate government authorities, anthropologists and committed private citizens. Among their tasks would be: working out 'reservation regulations', granting visitors' permits, and decisions on medical care, especially in connection with the prevention of contagious diseases and epidemics.

The conditions for creating a new reservation for the free Auca are extremely favourable:

They represent a small ethnic minority with absolutely no political significance.

Their demands with regard to land are comparatively modest.

They have expressed their wish for independence and have, with few exceptions, refused to be missionarized. They do not seek contact with civilization and want to be left in peace.

They live in geographical isolation. The nearest outposts of civilization are located many days' walk away. There are no roads leading to their territory.

Their land is of little economic interest. The Texaco-Gulf consortium has given up prospecting for oil on the Cononaco. No white settlers have to be expropriated, and no one will be making demands for compensation for land.

That the progress of western civilization does not always mean an improvement in the quality of life is a bitter realization. We see the foundations of our own way of life being threatened and are searching for ways out of the labyrinth we have constructed for ourselves. As we begin to doubt the motives of our meritocracy, our interest is awakened – perhaps too late – in primitive peoples whom we once so smugly considered backwards, but who know how to live in harmony with their environment.

The fate of the free Auca concerns all of us. The Auca are mankind's problem, not just Ecuador's. They have as great a right to live as the jaguar and the rhino. If we want to understand their world, we must listen to them. If they die out, their values and experiences will be irreplaceably, irrevocably lost, and we shall be the poorer for it.

At the moment, intolerance, ignorance and indifference are still allied against a solution to preserve their world; but the fatalistic view that the end of forest Indian culture is inevitable only speeds up the processes leading to their destruction. Integration or annihilation need not remain the only alternatives. There is another possibility for the Auca: survival in the tropical forests of their ancestors ... the way it has always been!

Nawanae's daughter Naentoca, the youngest member of the Auca group, is only a few days old. She is lucky that her life was spared. Ten-year-old Awancamo is Nawanae's only son. Since his birth she has borne only girls, and Naentoca's predecessor was killed at birth. The age-old custom of using infanticide as a means of population control has become rarer but is still employed by certain Indian tribes.

Epilogue

In the spring of 1980 the huts on the Cononaco were empty. For a few months the group had moved to another dwelling area about a day's walk away, north of the Cononaco. There the chonta palms hung heavy with ripe fruit, and the woolly monkeys were big and fat. They call the place Yuwitomi, Place of Fruit.

Back at the Cononaco, they were surprised in the middle of the year by the arrival of a group of twenty Auca from the reservation. These were the same people who two years earlier had been enticed to leave Titae's group and go to the Linguists' reservation settlement on the Rio Zapino. They had found nothing there of the paradise the missionaries had promised them; but they had paid for their guileless curiosity with the loss of their freedom. Unhappy with conditions on the reservation, they had succeeded in returning to their old home.

A few weeks later Titae died of an unidentified disease. His sister Miñimo and his son Caruae buried him in his hut. They broke his spear and blowgun in two and laid the pieces crossed on his chest. The Auca subsequently avoided the spot and the trails that led to it because of their fear of the invisible spirit of the dead.

On our most recent visit to the Cononaco in November 1980, we found all the huts on the right bank deserted and most of the trails overgrown. Caruae's family, with an infant girl Ñawanae had given birth to only a day before, and most of the new arrivals from Zapino were living in four new huts scattered in the forest on the other bank. All the rest, including Menga's, Apa's and Boca's families, had accepted an invitation from the Yasuni Auca about two months before and were at that moment either still with them or then staying in Yuwitomi on their way back. The reason for the invitation was probably connected with the marriage of Menga's daughter Wadi to Titae's son Oña and, shortly afterwards, of Apa's daughter Obi to Arabae from the Yasuní group.

The group of about 30 Auca living on the Yasuní River, among them the old shaman Nampawae, who is hammock-ridden with advancing muscle atrophy, is getting caught in the undertow of encroaching civilization. CEPE, the Ecuadorian petroleum concern, is invading their territory while, at the same time, Capuchin missionaries under the direction of Padre Alejandro Labaca see an opportunity of breaking the Linguists' monopoly on missionarizing the Auca. They are trying to win the Indians over with gifts, some of which are unfortunately articles of clothing. They have shown them how to use power saws and have traded rifles and ammunition for blowguns![1]

1 Juan Santos Ortiz, 'Los Ultimos Huaorani', Coleccion CICAME, Quito 1980.

The only Auca group that remains totally independent and remote from any contact with civilization is the one led by Taga and thus known as Tageiri; it is about 30 strong and nomadic. Thanks to its militant view of the outside world, it has managed to retain its independence. Intruders into their territory are met with spears, and three years ago the Tageiri made headlines when they attacked a patrol from an oil prospecting company working for CEPE, killing three of the workers with their lances.

The latest news from Ecuador brings new hope for the free Auca. The INCRAE (Instituto Nacional de Colonización de la Región Amazónica) has published plans for the establishment of a 4000 sq. km national park on the Yasuní, south of the Rio Napo. If this area were extended further south to the Cononaco by about 2000 sq. km, one of the fundamental conditions for the survival of one of the last sovereign Indian tribes would be fulfilled.